Grace:
The Choices We Make

To order additional copies, please contact us.
BookSurge, LLC
www.booksurge.com
1-866-308-6235
orders@booksurge.com

SHAROND
RAGIN

Grace:
The Choices We
Make

A NOVEL

2003

Grace:
The Choices We Make

In my life I've been bless to have great family and friends. Whether good times or bad, we've always stuck together. This book is dedicated to them for their love and support. A special dedication to Francine for her unbelievable patience and understanding. I love you.

This year I start to take form
Either as God's extension or as eyes that shine in the dark
This year I fight back and offer no excuses
opposition crushed and family nourished the year of the gladiator
-- Yinka Dare

IN LOVING MEMORY OF YINKA DARE
1972--2004

CHAPTER 1

Grace slowly opened her eyes, hoping something—anything—would be different. But the red glow from the bare light bulb in the corridor told her nothing had changed. She was still in prison, sprawled on a hard mattress in a gloomy eight by ten cell. She'd traded her Prada shoes for plastic sandals, a bubble gum pink Dolce & Gabbana suit for an orange jump suit. Instead of a sexy man in her bed, she had a female cellmate who snored and passed gas like a truck driver.

Another day would soon begin, almost exactly like the one before. Except today she would have a visitor.

Lisa Chang parked her five year old Taurus in the visitors' lot outside the prison and checked her reflection in the rear view mirror. Her sleek black hair was perfect. Her linen suit looked expensive, though she'd bought it in a consignment shop. She knew Grace was fashion conscious, so looks *did* count during this visit. She would leave nothing to chance.

Her purse went inside the trunk, because she already knew the guards wouldn't let her bring it inside. Next, she opened her attaché case and rechecked the contents: legal pad, pencils, tape recorder, and a contract. Calm and controlled. Easy does it.

She'd spent weeks arranging this visit with the elusive Grace Johnson. The next two hours could make or break her career as a journalist.

The prison complex looked even more desolate and frightening than she'd imagined. A water tower, a steam stack, and rows of brick and cement buildings were surrounded by tall fences topped by coiled razor wire. Tiny patches of grass seemed out of place amid the brick and concrete. Each building had a flat roof and rows of tiny, narrow windows.

At the first checkpoint a guard looked inside the trunk of her car and peered throught the windows into the back seat. They handed her a map and directions to the women's prison, which looked slightly less intimidating than the men's area. The women had more grass and an exercise yard with shaded picnic tables.

After an excruciating thirty minute wait, Lisa stood in line to pass through the metal detector and enter the visiting area—a dreary, cavernous room with wire-covered windows overlooking a concrete yard.

Lisa found her assigned table, a metal structure with the legs bolted to the floor. The matching bench was also fastened down. Everything in the room, including the furniture, was painted the same hideous shade of institutional gray.

Lisa removed her jacket and folded it on the bench, then placed the tape recorder beside her left elbow. She arranged the legal pad in front of her with a pencil atop it and waited with her hands folded. Stay calm. Stay focused.

Women and children occupied most of the other tables, with a few men scattered here and there. The children were subdued, clinging to their families, and Lisa surmised most would soon see their mothers. A sliding metal door rumbled open and the inmates filed in one at a time, reminding Lisa of a bizarre beauty pageant Each woman paused inside the door and looked hopefully around the room, then rushed to the appropriate table. They exchanged quick hugs with the visitors, monitored by guards and the cameras mounted in each corner of the room. One woman winked at Lisa, whistled at her, and then licked between her fingers. Lisa looked away, angry at herself for blushing.

Lisa recognized Grace right away from the courtroom and pictures in the newspapers and tabloids. She was stunning, even without makeup. Her brown eyes turned up slightly at the corners, giving her a vaguely oriental look. She had perfect eyebrows, full lips, and a ready smile for the other women. Tendrils of black hair curled around her face, her skin was flawless. In the uniform—faded jeans and a work shirt—she resembled an actress playing the role of a prisoner.

Lisa waved, motioning Grace to her table. Grace took her time, stopping to greet other prisoners and their families. The women seemed genuinely fond of her. Finally, she reached the table and slid onto the bench opposite Lisa. Grace folded both hands in front of her and met Lisa's eyes She didn't speak.

Lisa took a deep breath and began. "Thank you for seeing me, Grace. I know you've turned down visits with other reporters. I promise I won't waste your time."

"All I've got is time," Grace said. Her voice was so soft Lisa had to lean forward to hear.

"True. And I don't want to waste it. I know you've turned down other book offers, but I think you should consider mine. I've studied and researched your case from the beginning—I was in court every day and handled the story for my paper. I've lined up a respectable publisher and they offered a generous advance."

Grace shook her head. "I don't need money, you know that."

"I do. But perhaps you'd like to donate your share of the profits to some special cause."

Grace didn't answer, so Lisa rushed on. "Your story is unique and people want to know about you, Grace."

"Well, those people are either crazy or sick. You should be writing about some of these other women. Grace pointed to a skinny inmate with lank hair who held a couple of little girls on her lap. The children clung to her neck as though they'd never let go. "That woman killed her abusive husband to save her daughters, and now she's in prison while his family is raising her girls."

Grace gazed around the room. "This place was built for 150 prisoners and it houses 300. Most of them need help getting their lives together, not prison. And what's happening to their children while they're in here?"

Lisa hid her impatience. This wasn't going the way she'd planned, but she would not be sidetracked. "People want to know why you hired an expensive lawyer who said he could get you off, and then you pled guilty."

"I am guilty," Grace whispered.

"Okay. And so was O. J. if you ask me. But most people would rather not go to prison, whether they're innocent or guilty. That's why we have attorneys."

Grace shrugged, still watching the woman and her children.

"Think of it this way. What if your story could help someone else, keep another woman from making the same mistakes? Would that change your mind?"

Grace looked thoughtful. "Now that's a different way to look at it. So this book—I'd have the final say on what you write?"

"Of course. I brought a contract for you to read." Lisa slid a document across the table and their hands touched for a moment. "Maybe you'll want to have your attorney look this over."

Grace shook her head. "I was a legal secretary. scanned the document, raised her eyebrows. "Movie

"Why not? This story could go all the way." her ace. "Halle Berry—I see her playing your role."

Grace reached across the table and turned on the tape recorder.

Some people say money is the root of all evil. Is it? NO. But will it change you? Well, if it changes your lifestyle, then I think so. At least it worked that way for me....

One year earlier

Grace opened one eye and squinted at the clock radio on the pine table beside the bed. Six fifty nine. She had sixty more seconds of bliss before the music switched on and her day officially began. Dajour was already in the bathroom—she heard the toilet flush and water running in the sink. Moments later he came into the room, leaned over, and kissed her on the cheek.

"Mmmmm, you smell nice," she murmured. "I love that new after shave."

He pulled away. "I'm gone, baby. You have a good day."

Dajour was 255 pounds of pure man, with broad shoulders, smooth mocha skin, and intense green eyes. Just thinking about him made goose bumps stand up on her arms.

Loud music blared from the clock and Grace slapped the pause button, giving herself another ten minutes. She sat up, dragged the phone into bed with her, and dialed the office.

"Goldberg, Franklin and Associates. Cheryl speaking. How may I help you."

Grace prepared her best calling-in-sick voice. "Cheryl, I won't be in today." She stuck one finger down her throat, making herself cough. "I'm having another allergy attack."

Silence.

"I'm sure I'll be fine by Monday."

"I see." Ice dripped from Cheryl's voice. "Well, you'd better be here bright and early on Monday, Grace."

"I'll be home all day, resting in bed. Call me if you need anything." Grace hung up the phone and gave herself five seconds to feel guilty. Then she lunged out of bed, turned the radio on full volume, and headed for the shower.

In the bathroom she plugged in the curling iron, spent a few minutes under the hot water, splashed on a decent amount of perfume, and then dried her hair. It was PMS week, and she felt like a beached whale—bloated all over, with puffy circles under her eyes. Even her hair looked fat.

She selected a pair of tight jeans, red sandals, and a red tube top that hugged her chest. At least the PMS made her boobs look bigger—and the jeans worked as long as she didn't have to sit. She sang "How Will I Know" with Whitney Houston and put on her make up, taking plenty of time so it wouldn't look like she was wearing any.

Bypassing the kitchen to avoid feeling guilty over last night's dishes in the sink, Grace grabbed her purse and headed out the door.

Dajour strolled into the coffee shop and paused to look around. Although he'd arrived a few minutes early, Roxanne already occupied a corner booth, the furthest one from the door. She rested her head on her palm, her elbow on the table. Roxanne was a twenty-two year old graduate student working on her MBA while trying to start her own business. He's met her in a coffee show a few weeks earlier.

She smiled from behind the menu as he slid in across from her. He squeezed her hand. "Hey, thanks for meeting me. I know it's early, but this is the only time I can get away."

Roxanne raised one perfect eyebrow. "It's really no problem, Dajour. I'm a morning person—remember?"

"Yeah, I do remember. What are you having?"

"Just coffee for me. I ordered a number 6 for you."

Dajour waited while the waitress filled his coffee cup, then he relaxed in the seat and smiled at Roxanne. "So, did you find us a nice vacation spot?"

"Not yet, but I'll let you know the minute I do."

"Good." He leaned forward. "Roxanne, this is important. Grace can't know anything about it."

A few seconds of silence passed. "I have everything under control."

"Roxanne, I'm serious."

She gave him a sly smile and signaled for the check. "My lips are sealed."

Grace regretted wearing the sandals after she'd walked a few blocks and the first blister formed on her little toe. She was heading for a neighborhood deli with a cell phone pressed to one ear, dodging irritable commuters, mothers hauling their kids to daycare, and older kids walking to school.

"No, I cannot hold! You asked me to hold ten minutes ago. I'm on a cell phone, damn it! I can't be using up all these minutes on hold. Let me speak to your...hello? Hello?" Grace held the phone away from her ear and considered throwing it into the street. She'd just been hung up on—again.

"Watch it!" a teenage boy wearing a Paradyse Records backpack nearly took her head off when he swung around suddenly. Grace stepped over a pile of dog poop and hit redial on the phone. This was urban warfare, and she was a pro.

"Yes, Grace Johnson. I don't know exactly when, but it was like two months ago. What do you mean you don't have me in the computer? Okay, then maybe I booked it under Dajour Wright. Yes, W. R. I. G. H. T. Uh huh. No? Well, then how about you put me in the computer NOW. Hello? Hello? Shit!"

The battery was dead in her phone. She'd have to use the pay phone at the deli, but at least she could get a cup of coffee, read a magazine, and rest her sore feet. Marathon shopping was not for the faint of heart. Her favorite deli was just ahead, in the middle of a row of storefronts, sandwiched between a gift shop and a bookstore.

Unfortunately, the place was packed with coffee-starved commuters who'd formed a line stretching out to the sidewalk. Grace shoved her way inside and opted for the fruit drink section, which was less crowded. She grabbed a bottle of papaya juice and joined a line in front of the cashier, where a sign behind the counter advertised a grand prize of $40,000,000 for the lottery.

Grace opened the juice and sipped it. Three people in front of her were buying lottery tickets, each more irritating than the last. The first woman insisted on using exact change and counted out twenty cents worth of pennies. Next, an elderly man couldn't remember his numbers and had to search his pockets for a note. Finally, the woman ahead of her decided to write a check for five dollars. Grace was on the verge of wringing someone's neck when the old woman behind her spoke up.

"Baby, how come you ain't playing the number?"

"I don't gamble, Ma'am."

"Not even for forty million dollars?" The woman clutched a list of numbers in one hand and a wad of bills in the other.

"Everyone in this store has a better chance of being struck by lightening than winning the lottery."

The man behind the counter called, "Next!" and everyone moved forward a step. Like a bunch of sheep, Grace thought. The old woman lost her balance and grabbed onto Grace's arm. Her fingers were like claws, digging into the flesh. Grace winced and pulled away, steadying the woman before she let go.

The woman said, "But at the same time, everyone in this room has a chance of being struck by forty million dollars. Go on and buy a ticket, girl."

Grace shrugged. "Ah, why not?" She set her drink on the counter.

"Is that all?" the clerk asked.

Grace smiled at the old woman, who winked at her. "I'd also like a lottery ticket."

The clerk passed her a slip of paper and a stubby pencil. "Are you picking your numbers?"

"No, you pick it for me." She slid the paper back to him. Moments later the machine spit out a ticket and Grace slipped it inside her purse.

"Good luck, baby," the old woman said.

"You too!" Grace answered. She paused to throw her juice bottle in the trash and nearly collided with Cheryl, who'd just come in the door.

Wearing a tailored pants suit, flawless makeup, and a single gold stud in each ear, Cheryl was the perfect upwardly mobile executive. Her smile dripped sugar. "Grace! You look so healthy. What kind of water have you been drinking since this morning? Can I have some? Looks like you've got that allergy thing under control."

Grace's first impulse was to slink out the door, but she was trapped between Cheryl and a rack of potato chips. She took a deep breath and told the truth. "Look Cheryl, I had a lot to take care of today—stuff sprang up at the last minute. Dajour's having a birthday soon, and...."

"Save the BS, Grace. You're an adult and you and I both know the excuse game was played out in high school." Cheryl stepped aside to let the old woman pass. "I don't care what you do. You're the one who has to worry about keeping her job, not me."

Grace shrugged and headed for the door. "See you later."

But Cheryl always had to have the last word. She raised her voice. "Knowing you, on Monday you'll call in dead. Your days are numbered with the company, Grace. I suggest you report to work in one hour if you plan on keeping your job."

Grace slunk out the front door, hearing chuckles from the other customers. "Cat fight!" one of the men called after her.

CHAPTER 2

Exactly sixty five minutes later she entered the office and hurried toward her desk. Goldberg, Franklin, & Associates, an immigration law firm, was deeply conservative, so she had to rush home and change into a dress. No one entered the office in jeans, and even the cleaning lady dressed up. Grace worked in small office at the rear of the room and actually had a window—her only perk for three years of virtual slavery as an administrative assistant to one of the attorneys.

Her desk was exactly as she'd left it—cluttered, but organized. She had her own system and it worked. Grace turned on her computer and settled in the chair with a sigh. She was here, she might as well do something productive.

Janet appeared in the doorway holding two cups of coffee. "Grace, what were you thinking? Are you trying to get fired? We're supposed to have that project ready by Monday and you didn't bother to show up for work." Janet nodded toward Cheryl, who was on the phone, watching them while she carried on a conversation. "Her Highass is not having a good day."

Grace accepted the coffee and took a gulp. "Janet, I'm sorry, but I have so much to do and this was the only day I had. The hotel never booked the room for Dajour's party and they won't let me book another one. I've invited everyone we know, and now I'll have to cancel and plan something else." She dabbed her face with a napkin. "I completely spaced the project." Grace wondered if this was early senility. She really *had* forgotten the project and now it was too late to catch up—unless she came in on Saturday, which wasn't going to happen.

Janet glanced at the papers on Grace's desk. "Don't worry about it. We'll figure something out."

Cheryl's voice rang out. "So, Grace, you're here at work now, but you're still not working. What's wrong with this picture?"

Grace slammed the mug down, sloshing coffee on her desk. "What's the situation, Cheryl? I'm here, aren't I? You said be here in an hour, and I'm here. We're discussing the Ames project. What more do you want?"

"I want you to stop running your mouth and do your damn job for once."

Janet gasped and ducked out of the office. Grace felt her temples throb. It felt like someone was tightening a rubber band around her forehead. She slowly rose from her chair and faced Cheryl, but before she could unload, Janet grabbed her arm. "Grace! Come on, Grace. Let's go."

Grace pulled her elbow free. "Cheryl, what are you talking about? I think I speak for everyone when I say you can point to any person in this office and they work ten times harder than you."

Janet shook her head and put her index finger over her lips. By now, every clerk in the office had stopped working to watch the show. Grace felt a dozen pair of eyes on her, but she didn't care. "All you do all day is run your mouth, sit on your ass, and polish your damn nails instead of getting anything done," she added.

"You know why you feel like that Grace?" Cheryl asked.

Grace glared at her.

"Because you and damn near everyone else in this office needs a baby sitter, that's why. Now if I were you, I'd get back to work before I send you home."

For a moment Grace couldn't get her mouth to work. She unclipped her earrings and took them off. "Bitch, you don't have that kind of authority around here. Who do you think you are, talking to me like that?"

Cheryl threw back her head and laughed. "No need to get ghetto, honey. If I want to send you home, I'll send you home—for good."

"That's fine." Grace took a huge breath, walked to her desk, and swept everything off it with one arm, including the coffee. Half the papers landed on the floor and the others hit the waste basket, knocking it over. "Fuck this shit!"

The room was silent. Everyone looked down at their desks, pretending to work, and Janet scurried back to her cubicle. Grace strode past them all, heading for the front door.

Her grand exit was ruined when she reached the front lobby and realized she'd left her purse behind. She called Janet from the lobby phone.

"Can you sneak into my office and get my purse when Cheryl isn't looking? I'm still downstairs."

Janet wasn't thrilled, but she agreed. Grace flirted with the security guards at the desk and ten minutes later Janet stepped off the elevator.

"Girl, you sure can make a scene! I thought Cheryl would have a stroke when you knocked that stuff off your desk."

"Tell me about it! I don't know what came over me, but I almost threw my coffee at her." Grace was feeling rather proud of herself.

"Right after you left, Mr. Franklin came in, asking what happened. Cheryl's still in his office." Janet handed Grace her purse. "I'd better get back before they notice I'm gone. I'll call you tonight."

Janet grinned all the way back to the office. Cheryl was waiting in her cube, looking mad and worried at the same time.

"Janet, you can't wander off like that. Where've you been?"

"Grace forgot her purse. Can you believe it?"

"Good riddance," Cheryl snapped. She perched on the edge of Janet's desk, swinging one plump leg back and forth. "Now about that project—"

"I'll have everything ready by four o'clock, but I'd like to present it Mr. Goldberg myself so I can explain the details." *And take credit for the whole thing.*

Cheryl frowned. "That's not the way we usually do it."

"Well then, maybe I won't have it ready after all. This is very complicated, and without Grace's help...." She concentrated on her computer screen, giving Cheryl time to think this through and come to the right decision.

Cheryl bit her lower lip, obviously trying to choose between not having the project done on time versus sharing the glory.

"All right. Get it done by four and we'll go in together. But you keep your mouth shut until I tell you to speak." Cheryl marched back to her desk and Janet started printing the first draft.

Actually, Grace had already done most of the work on their project, and Janet knew she could add the finishing touches in less than an hour. She'd then put her own name on the report and personally deliver it to Mr. Goldberg.

About time she got credit for something. After working at the firm for 6 months, she was tired of seeing Grace land all the plum jobs. And Grace didn't seem to lift a finger half the time. Sure, Grace was smart, beautiful, and articulate—but so was Janet, plus ambitious. She'd set a goal to double her salary within 6 months. If Grace didn't stop messing around, Janet figured she'd meet her goal sooner than expected AND take Grace's job. In fact, by Monday morning she might be moving her shit into Grace's office.

An hour after storming out of the office, Grace still hadn't made it home. Once the adrenaline stopped pumping through her system, she got scared. This obviously meant the end of her employment with Goldberg and Franklin, and she could hardly ask for references. Much as she hated working for those tight ass lawyers, they paid her well and kept her in new clothes.

She wandered downtown, window shopping outside the department stores. How would it feel to purchase a diamond studded Rolex instead of a Seiko? How about wearing Prada shoes instead of imitations? Or buying furniture from the best stores instead of unfinished pine she had to paint?

Grace sighed, looking at the glittering merchandise. She'd never been poor—Daddy was a mailman and Mama taught fourth grade, but with six kids to raise they couldn't afford many luxuries. Her parents always worried about money; fretting over the monthly bills, saving coupons, looking for bargains. Just once in her life she'd like to have enough money. In fact, she wanted *more* than enough.

Catching her reflection in the store window, Grace realized her hair was a disaster. Weeks had passed since her last haircut, and the ends were a frizzy mess. Why hadn't she noticed?

"Cut if off," she told Shareen. Every head in the beauty shop swiveled her way, but the other women quickly returned to watching a soap opera on the TV set.

Shareen, the drama queen, posed with a pair of mean looking scissors "Are you sure about this?"

"I'm sure." Grace stared at herself in the mirror. "It's too much trouble curling it every morning and I've got better things to think about than hair."

"I hear you, girlfriend," Shareen said. "But it'll take a long time to grow back."

"That's okay." Grace thumbed thorough the People magazine on her lap until she found a picture of Halle Berry. "This is how I want to look. Can you fix my cheekbones too?"

Shareen snorted. "Not without plastic surgery, but we can do the haircut." She rubbed a clump of Grace's hair through her fingers. "What have you done to this? It feels like dead grass. Come on back to the sink. We're gonna give you a deep conditioner, and then I'll hook you right up."

Grace obediently followed her to the sink, leaned back in the chair, and fitted her head against the gap. Rather than stare at Shareen's armpits, she closed her eyes and relaxed beneath the warm water.

For some reason, Grace found herself remembering a summer vacation in the Smokey Mountains when she was eight. They stopped at a motel with a swimming pool, and then the whole family changed into their suits and rushed outside to swim. Even Pop wore swim trunks; she remembered the strong muscles in his legs, toned from walking miles every day with the mail.

"Don't go in the water until we get there," Mama called, but Grace was already out the door, running for the pool. Without a moment's hesitation, she flung herself into the water and sank like a rock.

She'd jumped into the deep end of the pool and had no idea how to swim, but for some reason Grace wasn't afraid. It felt safe and quiet under the water. Everything was so clear—the green and white tiles lining the pool, a wrinkled band aid floating in the water, blue and red marbles someone had dropped on the bottom. She held one hand out and spread her fingers, squeezed them into a fist to feel the water squirt out.

When her feet touched bottom she tried to catch a marble between her toes. Suddenly, a hand grabbed her swim suit and propelled her upward. She struggled, wanting to stay in the water, but her head broke the surface and Daddy was beside her, treading water, pulling her to the edge of the pool where a dozen people had gathered.

Mama wrapped her in a towel and carried her back to their room, alternately scolding and kissing her. "Child, you're too headstrong. If you go through life like this I don't know how you'll end up. You've got to think before you act."

Grace opened her eyes, realizing she still hadn't learned that lesson. Shareen massaged conditioner into the her scalp, slipped a plastic cap over her head, and settled her under a hair dryer for fifteen minutes. Grace looked down at her nails. They were all different lengths and her cuticles looked ragged. She could use a manicure, a pedicure, and a facial, but no way could she afford the full treatment. Someday...she told herself.

She left the salon with a new look. Next stop, a gourmet grocery store, where she bought a precooked lemon pepper chicken, a box of spicy ribs for Dajour, and a bottle of wine. She would not hang her head and act defeated over this job setback. Better days were ahead, she just knew it.

Back at the apartment, an incredible burst of energy propelled her into doing long-neglected housework. She did the laundry, folded it, and put everything away. She dusted and vacuumed the floors, scrubbed the kitchen counters, then set the table with candles and fresh flowers. Afterwards, she cleaned the bathroom, slathered a mud pack on her face, and soaked in the tub for half an hour. Dressed in a slinky skirt and a neon yellow shirt, she fixed dinner in her bare feet, listening to a Tracy Chapman CD.

When Dajour walked in the door she was sitting on the couch munching from a bag of salt and vinegar potato chips and watching Moral Court on TV.

"Hey baby, whatchu doing home so early? And what happened to all your hair?"

Grace ran one hand through her shorn locks. "Do you like it? I decided to try something different."

"Yeah, I like it a lot—makes you look like a teenager. I may be in trouble." He grabbed the potato chips and joined her on the couch. "Did that evil Cheryl let you off early?"

"Nope. I had a totally fucked up day."

"And Moral Court plus salt and vinegar chips is how you recover?"

Grace snatched the potato chips back. "Yes. It works for me."

Dajour wandered into the kitchen, following his nose. "Something smells fine in here." He let out a low whistle. "And look at that table. Must be my lucky day." He returned a few moments later carrying two beers. "What made today worse than any other?"

"Don't want to talk about it right now." Grace focused on the TV screen.

He picked up the remote, turned off the television, and took a seat next to her on the couch. She got up and started for the bedroom, but Dajour grabbed her wrist and pulled her back down.

"Grace, what did you do today?"

"I told you—nothing. Are you ready for dinner?"

Dajour leaned his head against the cushions and sighed. "Yeah, I see. But really, Grace, what happened?"

"I got fired, I think," Grace said in a small voice. She hugged a pillow to her chest, staring at the blank TV screen.

"What? What do you mean, you think? Did you or did you not get fired?"

"I don't want to talk about it." Grace stood, and this time Dajour didn't try to stop her. She wandered into the kitchen and tossed the empty chip bag into the trash.

"What did you do?" Dajour called.

"How do you know I did anything? Maybe they decided to downsize." She leaned against the doorway to the living room. The way Dajour stared at her, she felt like a bug under a microscope. His green eyes turned dark when he was upset, and at the moment they were almost black.

"After three years, you think I don't know you?" he asked.

"Okay, I called in sick today, did some shopping, and my supervisor saw me at the deli. I went in to the office, but she asked me to leave after we had an argument. Dumb bitch."

Dajour crossed his arms and she could almost read his mind. He was telling himself to stay calm, avoid a fight. "You really need to start thinking before you do things, Booby. We're struggling enough as it is. Why would you take a day off for no reason and then show up for work late, only to get sent home?"

She stormed back into the living room and flopped into a chair. "Dajour, I don't need your preaching to me after the kind of day I've had. You sound just like my mother." She softened her tone. "It's not like I got fired on purpose." She picked up her beer and took a sip, begging Dajour with her eyes to understand.

He stood. "The kind of day you had? All you had to do was go to work, and you couldn't even handle that."

Grace felt her temper rising again, and that tight band was back around her forehead. "It's bad enough I have to go outside and fight with everyone about what I am and am not doing right, but I'm damned if I'll come home and fight with my own boyfriend. Dajour, leave me alone." She fought back the tears, but couldn't hide the quiver in her voice.

Dajour came up behind her and put both hands on her shoulders. "Grace, hold up. Before this goes any further, I'm sorry. I don't mean to come at you the wrong way. I'm just saying, if you have a problem then we both have a problem." He stroked the side of her face.

Grace fished a tissue from her pocket and tried to get up, but he gently pushed her back. "Hold up, baby, sit down and let me finish." He moved in front of her and sat on a footstool in front of her chair. His long legs made it look awkward and Grace couldn't help smiling.

"Damn, who designed this furniture?" he muttered.

"I know that job you're working up there isn't easy; especially with Cheryl being there."

Grace nodded. "Those brothers at your construction site ain't half as tough as old Cheryl."

"You always hear me saying you've got to condition your mind so you can get where you want to be. I mean, you have to realize everything you're going through is temporary."

Grace frowned. She really didn't have the patience for a lecture right now, especially from Dajour, who could be incredibly self righteous. But there was no stopping him.

"Booby, understand that unless you have your own business, you'll always get caught up in society's way of doing things. For instance, take a three week vacation. What the hell is a three week vacation?" He grinned at her.

Grace shrugged. "I could use one."

"See, Grace, you're not feeling me. You're over there playing,"

"No, go ahead. I'm listening."

"Check it. You save money for three hundred forty-four days, just to spend it all in twenty-one days, and then you're back to square one—working long days and nights to pay the bills. Shit, if I didn't have a plan I'd be angry at the world too. That's why Cheryl's bent out of shape half the time." He reached for her hand. "Booby, don't be like that too."

Grace managed a smile. "Dajour, that works for you, but it's hard for me to do things that way. I'm more...spontaneous. If I plan ahead too much it feels like I'm shutting myself inside a box. I can't breathe."

His green eyes sparkled. "Wanna know the trick?"

She nodded. "Sure."

"I work harder."

Grace raised one eyebrow.

"Yup, I work harder and I sweat real hard, just to let myself know that if I don't—" he motioned with his hand, "this will be my reality until I'm sixty-five or dead, whichever comes first. The odds of me living to be sixty-five and collecting social security are about the same as hitting the lotto."

Grace just shook her head. "Most people accept the fact that they'll work until they retire at sixty-five."

"Tell you what. Let's make a deal. You always wanted to start your own interior decorating company, right?"

She nodded. "Yes, but that's just a dream."

"I'll pay the bills and take care of everything in the house and you can save money to start your own business," Dajour said. He massaged her hand and brought it to his lips.

Grace's eyes widened. "But..."

"The boss will give me all the overtime I can handle. And

whether you go back to this job or not, whatever money you make will go toward starting your own business."

Before she could answer, the phone rang. Dajour grabbed it from the coffee table.

"Hello? Hold on." He held the receiver down and covered it with his hand. "I think it's Cheryl."

"Just like I thought," Grace said. "Give it here."

"Hi, Grace. This is Cheryl. How you doin?"

What kind of a question was that, after Cheryl had nearly ripped her head off a few hours ago? Grace stood and paced the length of the room, wondering what was coming next. Cheryl didn't sound angry. She sounded...almost sweet. "I'm fine," Grace said.

"Grace, I'm calling to give your job back. But just know that if you even so much as breathe wrong, I'll fire you. See you Monday."

"See you—" the phone slammed in Grace's ear. "Monday."

Dajour swiveled on the stool, watching her. "What was that all about?"

"I got my job back." Grace grinned at him. "Guess they couldn't live without me."

He smiled and shook his head. "You are the luckiest woman I've ever met. Congratulations. Are you going to keep in mind what I said?"

"Yeah, thanks, babycakes."

"Alright, so I'm babycakes now?" Dajour slipped his arms around her and nuzzled her neck. "What have you got in mind for supper?"

CHAPTER 3

Janet checked her watch. She was ready fifteen minutes early, waiting for the doorbell to ring. She sipped from a glass of wine and stood by the window watching the street. Her new lace bra was giving her fits—it itched, but her cleavage had never looked better. In spite of her vow not to get excited about this date, she'd spent several evenings having her hair braided and paid a fortune for extensions. She spent another hundred on nails, a pedicure, and a facial.

Blind dates were a dumb idea—she knew it, but once again she'd let herself get talked into meeting a new man billed as Mr. Wonderful. Tonight's adventure was her next door neighbor's cousin. He owned a detective agency, which sounded exotic, collected antique cars, and owned a house in the suburbs. Then why was he still single? Janet knew it all sounded too good, but she'd said yes anyway. Nothing ventured, nothing gained.

She had a decent job, a little money in the bank, and a nice condo—but no one to share it with. She was tired of spending weekends alone, and totally burned out on the singles scene. For the last three years she'd been looking for the right man, but it seemed like all the good ones were already taken. Dajour for instance. If she'd seen him first, he'd be in her bed instead of living with Grace. But that game wasn't over yet, because Dajour hadn't married Grace and probably never would. In Janet's mind, he was still looking.

She used to think if a man didn't have good credit and pull six figures a year he wasn't worth her time. But lately, she'd been rethinking those standards. Men who had money seemed to measure life by how much they made, what kind of car they drove, and the size of their real estate holdings. They weren't accountable to anyone and the word *commitment*—forget it! There was a lot to be said for blue collar guys who got their muscles from hard work instead of buying them at the gym. After all, look at Grace and Dajour. He worked construction, but anyone could see the man was on his way up.

The doorbell rang. Janet left her wineglass on the table, smoothed her hair, and opened the door with a flourish. She stared up at the smoothest, finest black man she'd ever met.

"Janet?"

She nodded and sucked in her stomach, making it difficult to speak.

"I'm Mason Harris, Lisa's cousin. Sorry to come early, but I couldn't wait to see you. And you're even more lovely than Lisa said."

"Thank you," Janet said. She wanted to fall into his arms on the spot.

After dinner, Dajour helped Grace load the dishwasher before he settled in front of the TV to watch a game. Grace answered the phone when it rang, thinking it was Janet calling to gossip about the office.

"Grace?" Mama asked.

"Hi, Mama. How's it going?"

"We've had a rough day. Your Daddy's confused again and I had a hard time keeping him inside. I went to the bathroom and when I came out he was gone. I found him in the back yard trying to light the gas grill. Lucky he didn't blow himself up." She sighed. "He wouldn't take his pills either. I finally gave him some whiskey and he went to sleep."

Grace lay on the bed twisting the phone cord through her hands. Daddy had Alzheimer's disease and her strong, vital father was becoming an empty shell right before their eyes. "Is there anything I can do, Mama?"

"I wonder if you and Dajour could stop by tomorrow and put some new locks on the doors. If he puts a lock up high, then Daddy can't reach it."

"I'm sure Dajour will do that. We'll stop at the hardware store and then come on over. Maybe you and I can do a little shopping. Are you up for it?"

"Oh, you bet I am. And how's that job of yours?"

"Just fine, Mama. You know I do good work."

"Yeah, baby, and I also know what those lawyers are like."

"I can handle lawyers, but one of the supervisors is a total—well, you know. I swear Cheryl's got an iron rod stuck up her butt."

Mama chuckled. "I can just see that in my mind. What do they call it on Oprah—overcompensating?"

"Something like that," Grace said.

They talked for a few minutes more, and then Grace opened her laptop, and logged onto the Internet. The Ralph Lauren bedspread she'd been lusting after was still on sale, and this time she bought it—to celebrate getting her job back. The spread would match the drapes in their bedroom, completing a set she'd started buying several months ago. Decorating was her passion and they lived in a great apartment for it, with tall windows, polished wood floors, and high ceilings.

Three years earlier on a blustery spring day she'd stood outside the building, thinking it was beautiful. She'd just hired on with the law firm and still lived in a hideous studio apartment with a cantankerous two-burner stove and a refrigerator that hummed twenty four hours a day. Because she was looking for a real apartment, the For Rent sign outside the brownstone caught her attention.

The front door was open, so Grace stepped inside. Dry wall dust coated every inch of the foyer and her shoes stirred a cloud of white powder that clung to her black pants. The treads on the stairs were worn and the banister wobbled, but she kept going, drawn to the second floor by the sound of hammering.

Ten foot ceilings, exposed brick, and a southern exposure, she told herself, peering into the first apartment. Plus, it was only ten minutes from work. She wandered through the rooms, picturing African paintings on one wall, her grandmother's antique quilt on another. She'd hang plants in the windows and upholster the window seat with bright fabric.

The hammering stopped. Seconds later a man rushed out of the kitchen and crashed headlong into her.

"Oh!" Grace staggered backward and caught herself. The purse strap slipped off her shoulder, letting her Coach bag fall into a bucket of nails.

It was Dajour, looking so tall and handsome that Grace was speechless. "Sorry about that!" As he retrieved the purse and placed it back on her shoulder, his hands left a dusty print on her jacket

"Now look what I've done!" He tried to brush away the dust, but it only made things worse. They both laughed and he handed her a clean handkerchief from his pocket. Grace still hadn't spoken, but her mind was churning. She'd already noticed he wasn't wearing a ring and his muscular forearms were the color of coffee with a splash of cream.

Dajour grinned as though he could read her thoughts. "Are you here about the apartment?" he asked.

"Yes." She cleared her throat. "Yes, I am."

"The place won't be ready for a month or two, but they're signing rental contracts already. I'll hook you up with the owner. Make sure they promise to spray for bugs before you move in. I just saw a spider bigger than my hand."

Grace looked around wildly.

He laughed. "I'm just kidding. But you know how it is with these old buildings. Bound to be a few bugs here and there."

Before she left the building, Grace had signed a rental contract *and* made a date to meet Dajour for coffee. After a whirlwind romance they moved into the apartment together and had lived there ever since. Dajour found a better job with a construction firm and got promoted to supervisor, and Grace slowly moved up the ladder at Goldberg, Franklin, & Associates.

Grace closed the computer and snuggled next to Dajour on the couch, leaning her head against his shoulder. They were doing okay, she thought.

Mason invited Janet to a cocktail party thrown by one of his clients in a ritzy hotel. They cruised downtown in a new Thunderbird convertible, black with white leather seats. He handled the car with ease, weaving in and out of traffic, yet courteous to other drivers. Another plus.

"This is a great car," she said. "Did you just get it?"

He glanced over at her and smiled. "About three months ago. It's got a 3.97 liter, 32 valve V8 engine, 280 horsepower, and it's beautiful to look at. What more could a man ask for?"

"Sounds good to me," Janet said.

"You're damn right it's good. Watch this." He pushed a button and the convertible top slid back, exposing the night sky above their heads. "Only 20 seconds to raise or lower the top." He handed her a red silk scarf from the glove box. "Put this on so you won't muss your hair."

Janet admired his clothes. He looked casual, yet elegant, in khaki pants and a cashmere jacket. She was a bit overdressed by comparison, but he didn't seem to mind. She reached behind her and tugged at her bra, which insisted on riding up in the back.

The party was in full swing when they reached the hotel. The company had reserved a large conference room, complete with a free bar and a band. They found a table near the dance floor.

"May I get you a drink?" Mason asked.

"I'd love a glass of wine," Janet said, looking around the room. She hadn't overdressed after all. Mason was the only man not wearing a suit, but that only made him seem more confident.

"Red or white?" he asked. Another plus—at least he knew the difference.

"White Zinfadel, please."

"I'll be right back. Don't go away."

Janet had no intention of leaving. She found a breath mint in the bottom of her purse and popped it into her mouth, then focused on the music until Mason returned carrying two glasses of wine. He sat beside her instead of across the table.

"What do you do for this company?" she asked.

"I investigate potential new employees—on the executive level. I also look into possible theft. I'm sure you know that's a huge problem in the software industry."

"Of course. What about divorce cases, tracking down dangerous criminals, stuff like that?"

He laughed. "You've watched too many movies. I do a little surveillance work—mostly following errant husbands and catching them in the act. You'll have to come up and see my photo collection sometime."

"Anyone I'd recognize?"

"Oh, yes. You'll be amazed. But detective work is mostly drudgery, despite what you read and see on TV. I spend a lot of time gleaning information from the Internet and other sources." He paused and sipped his wine.

"Does it ever get violent? I mean, do you carry a gun?" The thought of it excited her.

"Sure. I have a concealed weapon permit and sometimes I deal with, shall we say, unsavory characters."

"Like gangster types?"

"I mostly work with white collar crime, but I have contacts everywhere. That's part of the job." He swirled the wine in his glass. "Enough about me. I understand you work for immigration attorneys. That must be interesting."

Janet described the job, embellishing her role at the office and trying to make it sound like a fascinating career choice. Mason listened and asked all the right questions, his gorgeous brown eyes focused on her.

"Would you like to dance?" he asked.

Naturally, he was perfect on the dance floor. His moves were strong and athletic, yet graceful, and he led with confidence. They danced several numbers and on the fifth she relaxed and rested her head against his chest, letting herself flow with the music. His muscular thighs brushed against her legs, he smelled wonderful, and his hands circled her lower back. Maybe, just maybe, this was the man she'd dreamed of.

Finally they wandered back to the table and Mason brought two more glasses of wine. By now they were holding hands and laughing together like old friends. Janet excused herself to visit the powder room, making it a fast trip because she didn't want to miss a second of his company.

When she returned another woman was in her chair. Mason looked embarrassed as he introduced them. "Janet, this is LaVona Wilson, a good friend of mine."

LaVona's smile was almost a grimace. "How nice to meet you. Have you two known each other long?" She glared at Mason, although the question was aimed at Janet.

"This is our first date." Janet sat across the table from the two of them.

"How lovely." LaVona stood and placed herself behind Mason, then whispered something in his ear.

He rose like a puppet on a string. "Janet, you don't mind if I dance with LaVona, do you?"

"Of course not." She watched them blend with the crowd on the dance floor. Mason glanced back at her with an apologetic wave, and then disappeared behind another couple.

Janet looked around the room, feeling conspicuous and out of place. A couple of women at the next table stared at her and whispered to each other. She knew they'd probably seen what happened. She spotted Mason's broad shoulders on the dance floor, and when he turned around LaVona's curves were plastered against him. He wasn't fighting it either. In fact, he pulled her closer and caressed her bottom with one hand.

Janet finished her wine, grabbed her purse from the table, and marched out the door. If she was lucky there'd be a taxi waiting outside the hotel. Fighting back the tears, she flagged a yellow cab and was just climbing into the back seat when someone grabbed her arm. She spun around.

It was Mason. "Janet, don't go! Let's talk this over."

As the cab sped away, she folded her arms and glared at him. "You'd better talk fast, because there's another taxi coming."

"I know I blew it in there, but I can't let you leave like this. Take a walk with me. Please."

He gave her such a pitiful look she almost smiled. "I'll give you fifteen minutes to make this right, then I'm outa here."

He walked beside her and she couldn't help remembering how well he danced and how they'd clicked from the first minute.

"I guess you could tell LaVona's my ex-girlfriend. She moved away and we haven't seen each other for a long time. That possessive streak of hers ruined our relationship."

"Uh huh. I didn't notice you fighting her off in there. In fact—"

"Hey, I admit we had fun on the dance floor for a minute or two, but then I remembered why we stopped seeing each other. And when I realized you'd left..." He shook his head. "I'm so sorry. I was rude, and I apologize."

Janet stopped and let him take her arm. "I guess I know how it is."

He steered her toward his T bird, parked across the street. "Let's start over and pretend this never happened. Why don't we go to my place for a glass of wine?"

Mason lived on the top floor of a high rise building with a fabulous view of the city. The entrance foyer had a marble floor, and the hallway led to sunken living room carpeted in white. Janet couldn't resist slipping her shoes off. The whole apartment was done in black and white, a sophisticated look with splashes of color here and there. African art books were spread across the marble topped coffee table and primitive tribal masks leered at them from the walls. Professionally decorated, Janet thought. The place was a bit contrived for her taste, but it did look masculine and expensive.

"Can you handle jazz?" Mason was turning knobs on his high tech sound system.

"Sure can." Janet settled in one corner of the black leather sofa and focused on looking relaxed. "I like your digs. That mask is almost scary." She pointed to a carved wooden mask displayed on a stand. The grimacing face was a deep mahogany color with a raffia headdress.

"Thanks." He settled beside her, but not too close. "I started collecting African art about a year ago and it turned into an obsession. That is a Chokwe dance mask and represents the incarnation of the female ancestor, the ideal woman."

"Whooee. She's one ugly sister. What about that horn thing?" Janet pointed to a reddish cone shaped object.

"That's a carved ivory horn from Benin, West Africa. It has the tree of life, a snake and different faces carved into it."

"They must be very valuable," Janet said.

"They're an investment. I believe in investments. "He smiled and took her hand. "Speaking of which, will you dance with me again if I promise to be good?"

His eyes drew her toward him and all the air in the room seemed to be disappearing. Janet nodded, not trusting herself to speak, and let him pull her to her feet. They swayed to the music, barely moving, letting the hot jazz wash over them. His touch brought a warm feeling to the pit of her stomach.

He kissed her forehead, her cheeks, and then her lips. "I know it sounds dumb, but I feel like we've known each other for a long time." He kissed her again. "Tonight I want to make you feel like the most desirable woman in the world."

Janet closed her eyes and smiled. Why not? He sounded good, he *felt* good, and she hadn't been with a man for over six months. She was starving for real affection and tenderness. She leaned against him.

Mason grabbed their wine glasses and led her into a master bedroom dominated by a king sized bed. Without missing a beat he unzipped her dress, picked her up, and gently placed her in the center of the white down comforter. By now his desire was obvious, but somehow he managed to keep control while he removed her bra and hung it on the headboard as though hanging a trophy on the wall. Next he attended to the task of removing her panties. Without so much as a single twist or knotting of the garment, he smoothly slid the red silk panties over her perfectly manicured legs and placed them on the floor. His execution was flawless. He never lost eye contact with her, and he seemed pleased at the amazement in her eyes.

Taking advantage of the moment, he teased her by slowly removing the rest of his clothing except for his silk boxer shorts. Waiting until her eyes begged to see more, he turned his back and without losing a beat, quickly removed the shorts. It was show time. Janet's mouth dropped open. She tried to look into his eyes, but it was hard not to focus on his impressive manhood.

They spent the next half hour exploring each other with hands and tongues. He kissed her eyes, her nose, her mouth, then her throat, then the pulsing spot at the base of her neck. He worked his way down her body, over her breasts, pausing to admire her pert nipples.

He whispered, "Baby, these are choice. I've never seen a woman with large breasts blessed with such small, succulent nipples." He continued down her ribs and across her belly. Through her body language Janet begged him to keep going, and he did—but slowly. The magic of his tongue brought her to release in a moment of such passion that she writhed on the bed and nearly threw him to the floor.

"Damn, woman! How long has it been?" He grinned at her, obviously pleased with himself.

"Too long." She held out her arms and pulled him on top of her. Now it was his turn.

The next morning Janet awakened early and rolled over in bed, stretching and yawning in hopes that Mason would awaken and make love to her again. He didn't stir, even when she blew into his ear. Finally she got up and took a shower, then slipped on a terry cloth bathrobe hanging on the back of the door and headed for the kitchen.

Mason's kitchen was large and sterile, almost like a restaurant. The counter tops were gray and pink granite, the cabinets glossy black. A six burner stove occupied the center of the room, with an array of copper bottomed pots hanging above the work area. After seeing a row of gourmet cookbooks lined up on the counter she wasn't surprised to find a fully stocked refrigerator.

By the time Mason awakened, she'd prepared omelets and bacon sizzled on the stove. Still-warm bagels were sliced and spread with cream cheese. She'd prepared gourmet coffee and two glasses of orange juice.

"Something smells good," he said, giving her a hug from behind. He looked cute and rumpled.

"I woke early and thought you might enjoy a nice breakfast." She flipped an omelet.

"I couldn't get back to sleep. I hope you don't mind."

"No, of course not." He sat on a stool at the counter and sipped his coffee. "Are you always so domestic?"

"No! My refrigerator's usually empty. That's why I decided to have fun in your kitchen."

"I'm glad you enjoyed it. I should be fixing you breakfast, not the other way around." Mason ate quickly and she sensed he was preoccupied, although he did keep up his end of the conversation. When they'd finished, he carried her plate to the sink, then returned and kissed her on the neck.

"How about a little dessert?" she asked.

He pulled away. "Baby, there's nothing I'd like better, but I have an early meeting. We'll just leave the dishes in the sink."

Janet sat up straight and smoothed her hair. "I've got a lot to do myself. I'll just get dressed and be off."

Fifteen minutes later, Mason called a cab, escorted her downstairs, and handed the driver a fifty dollar bill. "I'll call you soon," he promised.

In the back seat of the taxi, Janet dug through her purse for a cigarette, then realized she really didn't really want one. She sat there smiling, replaying the night in her head. At the moment it didn't matter if she never saw Mason again. She felt like a new woman.

CHAPTER 4

On Saturday morning Grace and Dajour drove to the suburbs to visit Mama and Daddy. Dajour brought his toolbox and they stopped by the hardware store to pick up a couple of sliding locks so Mama could secure the doors from the inside.

Grace's parents still lived in the house where she'd spent most of her life—a white clapboard home on a street where huge maples shaded the sidewalks. The neighborhood was going downhill as the old people either died off or moved away. Welfare families now rented the houses and hordes of little kids ran wild. Mama took it all in stride, befriending the single moms and playing grandma to their youngsters. Grace wanted them to move into one of those retirement centers, especially after Daddy got sick, but Mama wouldn't even discuss it.

Grace opened the back door and yelled, "Mama, we're here!"

Mama looked all washed out. She had on a faded housedress, no shoes, and her hair hadn't been combed—or washed. She hugged Grace, then Dajour, and led them into the kitchen. "Sit down and let me fix y'all something to eat."

"We're here to help, not make more work for you." Dajour set his toolbox on the floor and started running his big hands up and down the door frame.

"Now you've got to have a cup of coffee at least." Mama shoved Grace toward a chair and led Dajour to the kitchen table, which was covered with a red and white plastic tablecloth. Her salt and pepper shakers were chickens and the sugar bowl matched the ruffled curtains above the sink. Little in the house had changed since Grace was ten years old. Even the pink flowered dish towels were the same.

Mama poured coffee and brought a plate of cookies from the pantry. "I have to keep these hid from your father, 'cause he'd eat every last one and make himself sick as a dog."

"Where is Daddy?" Grace asked.

"Asleep, thank the Lord. He'll be down directly."

Grace met Dajour's eyes. "Mama, why don't you get cleaned up and I'll take you out to lunch. Dajour won't mind, will you baby?"

He nodded. "I'm just gonna be working on those locks. I'll keep an eye on Pops."

Mama's eyes brightened. "Well, if you're sure...."

Grace waited while Mama took a shower and then helped her fix her hair and put on a nice dress. She was shocked at how the dress hung loose on Mama's shoulders and hips.

"Are you eating, Mama? Look at all the weight you've lost."

"Course I am. But your father keeps me on the run and we don't get much sleep at night. He's awake all hours, roaming around the house."

"The doctor...." Grace began.

"The doctor don't know nothing. She gave him sleeping pills, but they make him worse. I've started giving him a shot of whiskey at night and I think that's gonna work."

"You tell me if it doesn't and I'll call that doctor myself." She paused. "Have you thought any more about moving?"

Mama gave her a look. "Now don't start that. We're staying right here."

Grace drove Mama's car, a powder blue 1978 Ford LTD with 50,000 miles on the odometer. It was like driving a boat, especially compared to her little Mazda. They stopped for lunch at a restaurant called The Three Pigs so Mama could order her favorite meal—beef Manhattan with a slice of coconut pie for dessert. A hideous mural of the three pigs, their houses, and the wolf covered one entire wall. It hadn't been changed—or cleaned—for at least twenty years.

"Remember when you had your parties here?" Mama asked, digging into a plateful of roast beef and gravy.

"Uh huh. You were pretty smart, having us roller skate 'till we were ready to drop, then come here for ice cream and cake."

"Sure saved a lot of wear and tear on our house. Remember that when you have kids of your own."

That was a loaded topic and Grace didn't take the bait. She ate her salad and watched the other patrons come and go. They were mostly retired people like her parents. Even the waitresses looked old.

"So how's it going with you and Dajour?" Mama asked.

"We're fine."

"He's a keeper, you know."

Grace rolled her eyes. "I plan on keeping him, so don't worry yourself about it. You've got enough on your plate with Daddy the way he is. Now finish up your pie and let's hit the stores."

Grace drove to the mall and took Mama into a department store. "No Walmart or Kmart clothes today," she announced. "You're getting some dresses that fit." She handed Mama an electric blue dress. "Now try that on and don't tell me it's too bright. The ladies in church will love it."

"Don't you sass me, girl!" But Mama carried it into the dressing room along with half a dozen others Grace selected.

It felt good, seeing the spark come back into Mama's eyes.

"That Dajour's a fine man," Mama called from behind the stall door. "When y'all gonna get married and give me some grandchildren?"

Grace rolled her eyes. "When he asks me, Mama."

"You *know* what I think about it."

"Yes, I do, Mama."

"Why buy the cow when you can get the milk for free?"

Grace pretended not to hear. They'd covered this ground a dozen times and she knew Mama was probably right. But it was too late now—she wasn't about to leave and Dajour knew it. She could only hope he'd propose to her in his own time.

When they got back to the house, Dajour had finished installing the locks and he and Daddy were in the back yard, sitting in the matching lawn chairs Dajour made them for Christmas. When Grace bent over and gave her dad a hug he backed away and looked at her with a blank stare. Her heart sank, realizing the day would soon come when he wouldn't know her. But this time his memory kicked in and he grinned.

"Hey, Booby! Welcome home. You been out with your Mama?"

Grace sat beside him and took his hand. He looked thin and his shirt had dried egg yolk crusted on the front. His socks didn't even match. Grace felt like crying. Her Daddy had always been a natty dresser and now he didn't care how he looked. She forced a smile.

"Wait 'till you see the clothes Mama bought. She's gonna be the envy of those women at church."

But Daddy had noticed a blackbird in the yard and didn't seem to hear. He stood and wandered toward the back gate.

"I put a secure lock on it," Dajour said. "He can't get out." He leaned across and patted her hand. "I know this is hard on you."

They stayed until Daddy fell asleep again and Mama said she was ready for a nap. Before they started home, Grace tiptoed into the bedroom and kissed Daddy's forehead. He slept like a child, innocent and carefree with the quilts tucked under his chin. "Bye Daddy. I'll see you soon," she whispered.

On Monday morning Grace arrived at the office feeling rested and productive. Cheryl nodded but didn't speak, and the air was definitely frosty. Grace considered rotating her desk to face the window so she wouldn't have to look at Cheryl, but decided that was too obvious. Instead, she kept busy on the computer and refused to acknowledge Cheryl's evil stare. Maybe the bitch would find someone else to torment.

Janet stopped by around ten o'clock. "Man, Grace, after your little episode from Friday I didn't think you'd be coming back." She perched on the chair beside Grace's desk.

Grace smiled. "It's a new day. Besides, I have my very own motivational speaker at home."

"I heard Mr. Goldberg came looking for you on Friday and had a fit when he heard Cheryl sent you home. You're the only one who knows what's going on with his cases."

"That's my job security," Grace said. "As long as I keep the attorneys happy Cheryl can't touch me."

"Girlfriend, you're smarter than you look. I came over to ask if you want to put in this lottery pool. The jackpot's up to 40 million dollars this week."

"No, I already bought my ticket." Grace stretched her arms, aware Cheryl was watching them but didn't dare say anything.

"So what are you afraid of—having too many lottery tickets?"

"I just don't like throwing away money like that. I really shouldn't have bought the one I have in my purse, but I let some old lady talk me into it."

"Suit yourself." Janet wandered off and Grace returned to her computer. If she finished Mr. Goldberg's project by noon she could take an extra fifteen minutes for lunch, which would drive Cheryl crazy.

Janet stuffed the lottery tickets into her purse and stared at the phone on her desk. Did she dare call Mason again? She'd already tried his apartment several times, repeatedly getting the answering machine. If he checked caller ID and realized how many times she'd called, then she'd *never* hear from him.

Damn it, he was supposed to call! Had she done something wrong? Or maybe she'd tried too hard and he sensed she was needy. Nothing scared men off like being needy. Just for luck, she dialed her own number and checked her messages. No calls since the last time she'd checked an hour ago. She pushed the phone away and clicked her mouse, bringing the computer screen to life. Okay, so this Mason thing hadn't worked out— so what? One of these days she'd find somebody else.

Dajour drained the last of his Pepsi and tossed the can into the trash bin with a perfect hook shot. He and Smitty were finishing their lunch break, sitting in the shade cast by a cement truck. The rest of the crew crowded around the lunch wagon buying drinks and sandwiches. Groups of men wandered off to eat in different locations around the construction site. A generator purred in the background.

"Damn! These sandwiches get worse every day." Smitty wadded what was left of a ham sandwich into a ball and threw it toward the trash can. "I can't believe what they charge for this crap."

"Ever thought of bringing your own food?" Dajour asked.

He carried a lunch box and brought stuff from home every day. It saved money, and he ate better.

"Too much trouble. I barely get here on time as it is. And Doretha likes to sleep late, so I don't ask her to make my breakfast—or pack my lunch."

They watched a Mexican crew arrive and begin unloading topsoil around the building's foundation.

"Man, I can't believe this thing is almost done," Dajour said. "Seems like it was yesterday when we first broke ground."

"May as well been yesterday. They don't build things like they used to. It took them damn near 100 years to finish that cathedral. This piece of shit we building'll be finished by next week. I tell you man, I never seen so much cardboard and fiberglass. And to think they wanna call this construction."

Dajour took a bite from his sandwich. "How's the wife, Smitty?"

A pair of fine looking women sashayed past, slowing their pace to look at the building. One of them peered at Dajour over her sunglasses.

"Oh, Doretha's fine. She might be sagging, but she has a lot of kick still left in her."

Dajour shook his head and smiled. "How long have you two been married?"

Smitty thought for a few seconds. "Thirty one years. I'm fifty years old and I married Doretha when I was nineteen." He grinned. "Four boys, ten grandchildren. Might be eleven, but my oldest son says he isn't too sure."

Dajour wiped his forehead with his arm. "That's wild, man."

"You tellin' me."

"No, I mean about the thirty one years. You know, being married to the same woman all that time.

Smitty shrugged. "I don't know. I guess you just get used to it after awhile."

"She doesn't make you happy?" Dajour asked.

"Don't get me wrong, youngblood. Smitty is a very happy man. I'm well fed, I get all the ass I want, got me a nice clean house and a family that loves me. Me personally, I can't ask for nothing else."

"I hear that."

Smitty leaned toward him. "Is everything going alright with you and Grace?"

"Yeah man, I'm thinking about marrying her, that's all."

Smitty nodded his approval and took a sip from his soda can. "Go for it man. Just be careful—they don't make women like they used to."

"Like buildings, huh?" They watched a scrawny looking kid push a wheelbarrow filled with scrap to the burn barrel and dump them in a pile.

"Just a second," Dajour told Smitty. He took a sandwich out of his lunch box, placed a ten dollar bill inside the wrapper, and carried it over to the kid.

As he came back, Smitty was shaking his head. "That Billy is one sick lookin white boy. Why'd you hire his sorry ass?"

"He's a good worker."

"Looks to me like drugs have done fried his brain." Smitty said. "Why you giving him money?"

"He's in rehab and I know he's hurting until his first paycheck. That's why he didn't stop for lunch—no cash for the lunch wagon."

Smitty grunted. "Now here comes real trouble." A young guy strutted down the sidewalk toward them, wearing baggy pants and a head rag. "Look at that Low. Never done a lick of work in his sorry life."

Low sidled up to them and gave Dajour a five. "S'up Day Day?"

"S'up, man?"

"Hey Smitty, can you spot me a dub?"

"Can I spot you a who? Boy, you know better than coming at me with that old gangsta' lingo."

"Come on man. I'm a little low right about now. Help a brother out 'til payday." He lounged against a sawhorse and wiped his face with a rag.

"You said the same thing last time. Matter of fact, you say that every time. Low, come to think of it, you owe me sixty dollars. What the hell happens to your paycheck?"

Dajour held one finger against his nose and sniffed.

"Nah, man. I don't mess wid that stuff. I'm good for the money."

"Yeah, well you better get me my sixty dollars for I whup your motha' fuckin' ass," Smitty said.

Dajour laughed. "He's right, bro. You owe it."

Low turned to Dajour with his hand out. "That'll be twenty dollars."

"Shit. You wild out your mouth."

"Day Day, I don't entertain nobody's kids for free. You want to laugh, you need to pay up."

"Go ahead man," Dajour said.

Smitty nodded. "Yeah, we was cool before you come along."

Another woman passed by on the sidewalk and Low swung his head to watch her. "Her ass so fat you can see it from the front." His extended palm turned into a fist.

Dajour gave him dap and Low wandered off, following the woman down the block. "Knowing him, he'll be asking her for money."

"Knowing him, he'll get it," Smitty added.

CHAPTER 5

Next Saturday evening Grace and Dajour relaxed in their apartment, getting ready to watch a movie they'd rented. Grace was in the kitchen making iced tea and Dajour sat on the couch with a bowl of popcorn.

"Hurry up with that tea so we can put the movie in," Dajour called.

"I'm coming." She poured their tea, put the pitcher in the refrigerator, and carried the glasses into the living room on an antique tray.

"Is Cheryl still on your back?" Dajour asked.

Grace giggled "Now she's on my nuts."

He stopped eating popcorn and gave her a look. "Say what?"

"Well, ya'll get to say it."

"That's because we have nuts to speak of."

She grabbed a handful of popcorn. "It's a figure of speech. You know what I'm talking about."

"So she likes your work?"

"She'll never like my work, but I decided to apply what we talked about last Friday at work for the past week. So far, so good."

"Told you so." Dajour returned his attention to the TV, where a slinky blonde wearing a tight red dress was drawing balls out of plastic bubble. The words POWER BALL popped up on the screen.

"Hey, baby, watch this. Did you know the jackpot's forty million."

"Are you watching the jackpot or those boobs?" Grace stood to carry her glass back to the kitchen and add more sugar. "As a matter of fact, I bought a ticket last Friday. Do you need more sugar in that tea? Mine's not sweet enough."

Dajour took a sip. "No, this is great. Just hurry back so we can put the movie in. And I'll take your fine boobs over hers any day," he called.

Grace dumped two spoons of sugar into her glass and stirred it, thinking about the old woman she'd met in the deli and half listening to the Power Ball announcer. "And the winning numbers are seven, two, thirteen, five, nine, three! The Power Ball number is five."

Grace froze, whispering to herself as he repeated the numbers two more times. She stood in the doorway, her mouth hanging open, staring at Dajour.

"What?" he asked. "Are you sick?"

She danced around the room, whooping and screaming. "Oh my God! Oh my God! I don't believe it!"

Dajour laughed. "Now you're throwing some kind of fit. What was in that tea?"

Grace grabbed her purse from the hall table and dumped the contents on the living room floor. She rooted through makeup, a cell phone, the check book, and finally held a lottery ticket in the air.

"I won! Oh my God, I won!" She kissed the ticket and held it toward the ceiling.

Dajour took it and read the numbers. He grabbed her in a bear hug and they danced around the room until the downstairs neighbor pounded on the ceiling. They both sank onto the couch, exhausted. Grace picked up the phone and started dialing.

"Who you calling?" Dajour asked.

"First Mama, and then my job. I'll leave a message on Cheryl's machine telling her I quit."

Dajour took the phone and hung it up. "You can tell your Mama, but I don't want anyone else knowing about this for awhile."

"Why not?" Grace frowned at him. "We could throw a helluva party."

"Haven't you heard what happens when people win the lottery? We'll be swamped with letters and calls from people begging for money. Relatives you don't even know will crawl out of the woodwork like cockroaches. The TV stations will be all over us. We'll never have minute's peace."

"The TV part sounds like fun," Grace said. "I've never been on TV."

"I say we play it cool for awhile. Don't tell anyone until we decide what to do next."

"But Dajour—" Grace stopped herself. Dajour was always sensible and nearly always right. "Okay, we'll do it your way. But I really need a new car!"

Dajour seemed amazingly calm. He went to bed early and was snoring by 11 p.m.

Grace couldn't even think about sleep. Her mind kept turning over what she'd do with the money. A grand house for her parents with a nurse for Daddy, new clothing, fine cars, her own business, a house in the country—everything she'd dreamed of was possible.

Dajour woke at 3 a.m. to go to the bathroom and squinted at her in the light from the street lamps. "You still awake, Booby?"

"I'm too excited to sleep," Grace said, stretching her arms. "There's so much we can do. Why don't we take a year off and just travel the world?"

"Sounds great." Dajour went back to sleep and she curled next to him, spooning her body against his back. His deep, regular breathing soothed her. She touched the lottery ticket under her pillow. She'd placed it inside a plastic bag and taken it to bed with them in case someone broke into their apartment during the night. Or worse yet, the apartment might burn down and forty million dollars would go up in flames. So she kept one hand on the ticket, just in case.

When she finally fell asleep, Grace dreamed she was inside a beautiful house, much like the mansion she'd dreamed of owning. The house was big and silent. Twenty foot ceilings were trimmed with gold leaf and glittering crystal chandelier hung above the entryway. A graceful, curved central staircase with a cherry banister led to the second floor. At first Grace almost ran through the rooms, planning how she'd decorate and furnish each one. She counted over 40 rooms in the house, including a wing of servants' quarters where the accommodations were small and depressing.

At the center of the house was an octagonal ballroom, the wooden floor polished to a high sheen. From the center of the room she watched a pale figure enter from the other side. It was the old woman from the deli, wearing a dress of gray satin. As Grace started toward her the woman vanished.

"Wait!" Grace called. She knew the woman wanted to deliver a message, but there was no sign of her anywhere. The house turned cold around her, as though someone had pumped refrigerated air through the windows.

For the first time Grace realized she was completely alone. She ran upstairs calling Dajour's name, darting in and out of the empty bedrooms. Finally she ran up a dark, narrow flight of steps to hide in the attic, terrified of a nameless presence that had entered the house. She heard it coming up the stairs, moving through the rooms she'd just left, sniffing the air for her scent. There was the thump of a footstep and then the sound of the other foot dragging. This continued all the way down the hall until IT reached the attic door. She'd left the door open. Cowering in a dark corner of the attic, she waited.

Suddenly as the walking reached the door a great wind rose from the stillness, the single light bulb above her head went out, and the door slammed shut.

Grace sat straight up in bed, trembling and covered with sweat. She had to take a deep breath, then another. Her heart was still racing and the hairs had prickled up on the back of her neck. She couldn't stop shivering. A cold breeze from the open window had slammed the bathroom door. She grabbed Dajour and held him close for the rest of the night.

After waiting in vain for Mason's call, Janet decided to take matters into her own hands. Not that she was madly in love or anything, but the man did fabulous things in bed and she wanted another round. Since he'd chosen to ignore her messages, she devised a way to run into him. After locating his office in the yellow pages, she drove by and cased out the area. A dry cleaning shop in the storefront next door would give her a perfect excuse to be in the neighborhood.

She called his office, pretending to be a prospective client, and learned from the secretary that Mason usually went to lunch around 11:30. Next, she left an armful of clothing at the cleaners one evening after work, though it meant driving across town in rush hour traffic.

After telling Cheryl a whopper about seeing the gynecologist, Janet left early for lunch and picked up her clothes at exactly 11:25. With two suits draped across her arm she lurked under the awning outside the cleaners, waiting for Mason to leave his building. If the plan worked she'd step out with her head down, run into him, and then act totally surprised.

She'd say: "Why Mason, I didn't expect to see you! How've you been?"

He'd give her that sexy smile and say, "Damn woman, you're looking fine. I've been meaning to call you."

"I've been so busy. Things are just now slowing down for me." She'd rearrange the clothes on her arm while glancing at the coffee shop across the street. He'd surely invite her to lunch, and after that....

A woman maneuvering a stroller bumped Janet's leg, interrupting the fantasy. She checked her leg and, sure enough, the left front wheel had ripped her panty hose. By the time she looked back at the building Mason was coming out the door.

Pull yourself together, girl. This is it!

He paused to hold the door for a woman. Out came LaVona, dressed to kill in a blue suede pants suit. Her breasts were practically hanging out of the low cut blouse. She paused in the doorway to kiss Mason on the lips. Moments later, the two of them sauntered down the sidewalk, arm in arm.

Janet sagged against the wall. *Ex-girlfriend?*

Grace had to wait almost a week before picking up her check at the state lottery office—an agonizing week during which she could barely concentrate at work. The TV stations speculated about who'd won the money, but she followed Dajour's advice and asked the lottery people not to reveal her name.

Finally, the big day arrived. She left the lottery office carrying a check with so many zeros she could barely read the total. The money went directly into her bank account—and Grace swung into shopping mode. First, a trip to Nordstrom, where a petite young thing helped her select a multitude of designer suits while trying hard not to stare. Then to Sak's for more clothing, from underwear to hats. None of it was on sale and not a single item came from the budget shop.

Driving through the streets in a taxi with the backseat crammed with shopping bags, she noticed the little deli where she'd bought the lottery ticket. On an impulse, she had the driver pull over while she went inside. She ordered an iced coffee and approached the sullen looking clerk at the checkout counter—the same man who'd sold her the ticket.

"Excuse me?" she planted herself directly in front of him.

He glanced at her, then went back to counting money in the register. "What can I do for you?"

"I'm looking for an old woman I met in here. She was all bent over and walked with a cane. She had on a gray dress and a black hat with a little veil—like women wear to church. Do you know who I mean?"

The man shrugged. "Don't think so."

Grace placed a crisp, new fifty dollar bill on the counter— something she'd seen done in the movies. The man folded the money and slipped it into his pocket. Now she had his attention.

"I wait on a lot of old people from the housing project down the block, but I don't know exactly who you mean. You want me to call you if someone like that comes in?"

"That would be great." Grace gave him her phone number and hurried back to the taxi. She was climbing into the backseat when she spotted an old lady with a cane hobbling down the street about half a block ahead of them.

"Take me up to that woman," Grace told the driver.

As they drew closer, the woman turned a corner with surprising agility. The driver paused for a red light, then made the turn. "Well, looks like we lost her." He slowed the car and idled along the curb. There was no one in sight.

"Well, I don't know where," Grace said. The entire block was vacant lots and boarded up storefronts.

"Do you wanna stop?" he asked. "I wouldn't advise it. This ain't exactly the best neighborhood."

"No, just take me home. It probably wasn't her." Grace leaned back in the seat and opened one of her bags to admire the silk nightgown she'd just purchased.

She bought Dajour a new wardrobe, but he wouldn't wear most of the clothing she'd selected. "Baby, I can't wear this stuff to work," he said. "I'll just ruin it."

"Well, you'll need better clothes when you start your own company," she told him. "Why don't you quit now and get started?"

"I need a little time," he told her. "I've been saving for years to start a company and all of a sudden somebody hands it to me on a silver platter. It's a big shock. And besides, I don't like taking money from you. "

"But it's *our* money," Grace said. Still, she'd opened the new bank account with only her name on it.

Dajour preferred to keep his five year old truck, but she paid cash for a silver Bentley GT Coupe and drove it home from the dealership by herself. She stopped at Dajour's construction site and tapped the horn. He strolled out to admire the car, followed by every other man on the job.

"Damn, baby, this is one bad machine. Pop the hood for me." He opened the front end and six men clustered around the engine, giving low whistles.

Smitty leaned inside the window and grinned at her. "You know Grace, people gonna think you're selling drugs if you keep flaunting your money like this."

Obviously Dajour had told at least one person about the lottery check. She shrugged. "Isn't that what money's for—to enjoy?"

Next, she bought new furniture for their apartment, redid everything in the kitchen, and had custom draperies made for the living room. Meanwhile, she was thinking about real estate.

"Dajour, we can buy any house we want. Just tell me what you like and we'll start looking."

He was sitting at the kitchen table reading the paper. "A swimming pool, a workshop, and a bathtub big enough for both of us at the same time. That's all I care about."

"Perfect," Grace said, jotting notes on a pad of paper. "I'll tell the real estate agent and they'll give us a list of properties. We can go house hunting over the weekend."

"But we'll have to commute," Dajour pointed out. "I like it here because you can walk to work and it's convenient to everything we need."

Grace rolled her eyes. He simply didn't *get* it. "Honey, I won't be working there much longer and you'll have your own construction business. We won't need this neighborhood. We're moving up in the world."

Dajour looked at her over the top of the paper. "I'll leave it up to you. Just remember, I'm happy anyplace as long as we're together."

Naturally, everyone at the office had noticed Grace's new clothes—and her attitude. Now she almost felt sorry for Cheryl and Janet, knowing they'd be stuck in dead end jobs for the rest of their lives.

Grace breezed into work on Monday morning and began sorting things in her desk. She'd planned to stay all day, but by noon she couldn't stand it any longer. She walked over to Cheryl's desk.

"I like your shoes," Cheryl said. "Where are you getting those new clothes?"

Grace shrugged. "Maybe I've got a sugar daddy."

"Well, whatever it is, you've been doing great work lately and I like your new attitude. If you keep this up, next year you'll be making fourteen dollars an hour."

Grace smiled pleasantly. "Cheryl, I quit."

"Say what?" Cheryl tilted her head to one side.

"I quit as of right now, today. No more work."

Cheryl crossed her arms. "No way. I'll need a written letter giving two weeks' notice and you'll have to work every day of that time. Otherwise, no reference."

Grace smiled again. "How about you notice I'm not here for two weeks?"

Cheryl sputtered, but Grace interrupted before she could speak. "See Cheryl, I really don't understand what the big deal is: you're always threatening to fire me on the spot."

"Fine, Grace. Just don't bother putting this job on your resume, because you won't get any decent references coming out of here."

"That's cool." Grace walked toward Janet's cube. "I'll be back later to get my things. I have some business to take care of right now."

Janet looked up from her work. "Grace, what's up?"

"I just quit—for real this time. Wanna go to lunch? It's my treat."

Janet was surprised when Grace took her to Claude's, an upscale French restaurant instead of the coffee shop where they usually ate lunch. A dozen well groomed patrons looked up from their food as the two women entered. Janet felt out of place in her pants suit, but Grace seemed right at home.

Sitting in a padded booth, Janet gazed around the rich,

earthy interior where the walls were deep red and the booths were decorated in hues of red, blue, brown, and eggplant. A waitress brought two menus that were approximately fourteen inches tall. Both women ordered spiced chai and the luncheon special.

Janet leaned across the table. "Grace, what's going on? All these new clothes, the Prada shoes, and now you quit your job. And how can you afford this place? Did you notice the prices?"

Grace sipped her chai. "What Prada shoes?"

"Grace! Do I look stupid?"

Grace giggled and held out one foot. "They are nice, aren't they!"

"Are you selling drugs?" Janet whispered.

Grace laughed.

"Did someone pass away and leave you money?"

The waitress brought their food and Grace began eating her pasta. Janet added salt to her food, bringing a scowl from the maitre de. "Somebody at the office said they saw you driving a new Bentley. I'll die if you don't tell me what's going on."

"I want to, but Dajour says I can't tell anyone."

"Gimme a break," Janet said. "Am I not your best friend?"

"You promise not to tell anyone?" Grace asked, winding angel hair pasta around her fork.

Janet pouted and rested her chin in one hand. "Do I look like the National Enquirer? Who would I tell?"

"Swear to God?"

"Grace, like I said—who am I gonna tell?"

"Okay." Grace took a sip of water, then a deep breath.

Janet stopped eating and waited.

"I hit that forty million dollar jackpot. I asked them not to reveal my identity, but it was me!"

Janet's mouth dropped open. "Stop lying, girlfriend! I've never heard such a story in all my life. People were staring at them, but Janet couldn't keep her voice down. "Your mama should wash your mouth out with soap."

"It's the truth, I swear."

"Oh my God! Was it really you?"

Grace looked around. "Shhhh. I got the Bentley to prove it."

Janet gave her a high five, bringing more stares from the other patrons. "So what are you going to do with the money?"

"Spend it."

Janet gave her a look. "You can do better than that."

"No, I think I'll invest it, buy my parents a new house, by Mama a car, and then get Dajour's mother a house and car. Maybe I'll finally get the old heifer to like me."

"Wow. What else?"

"I'll buy myself a house. Oh yeah, Dajour wants to start his own construction business too. That's the first thing we'll do with the money. After I help him start his business, I'll start my own interior design company."

"Cool. But you forgot something."

Grace took another bite and raised her eyebrows.

"You didn't say nothing about hooking a sister up." Both of them laughed and Janet watched Grace's face. "We're friends—how you gonna leave me out like that?"

"Don't even worry about it, I already got you."

"Just checking." Janet moved the food around on her plate, too nervous to eat another bite. This was her chance. Her eyes brightened as Grace reached for her purse.

"Matter of fact...." Grace said. She pulled out a checkbook in a leather holder, followed by a gold Cross pen.

Janet tried to look nonchalant, admiring a painting on the wall as Grace signed her name with a flourish and held out the check.

"Here you go."

Janet accepted the paper with trembling fingers and turned it over. She stared at the numbers, looked a second time, and burst into laughter. "Are you serious?"

"Well, you deserve it," Grace said.

"Grace, you just hit the lottery for forty million dollars and you have the nerve to sit here and write me a check for ten thousand dollars?" She laughed a little to soften the words.

Grace smiled back at her, oblivious. "Don't spend it all in one place." She tucked the checkbook back inside her purse and resumed eating as though nothing had happened.

Janet could almost feel steam coming out her ears. "You know, Oprah gave all her friends a million dollars, Michael Jordan bought Pippen a damn Ferrari or Lamborghini or something 'cause it was his birthday, and all I get is ten G's?"

Grace lifted her palms. "What?"

Janet clenched her fists below the table, forcing herself to laugh. "It's okay, I was just messing with you. Thanks, girl. You really didn't have to give me this."

"Please, it was nothing."

Your damn right it's nothing, Janet thought. She couldn't believe Grace would be so stingy, especially after all they'd gone through together at work. For a second she'd misread the zeros on the check and thought she had a hundred thousand dollars. This was heartbreaking. She almost wanted to tear up the check and fling it in Grace's face, but only a fool would throw money away.

Grace checked her watch. "Your lunch hour's almost up."

Janet wiped her mouth with the linen napkin and signaled

for the check, which she had no intention of paying. "By the way, did you ever get that birthday thing sorted out?"

"No, but I'm not worried about it now. We'll just think of something else to do. Hell, I could buy the entire hotel if I wanted to."

"You're a trip" The waitress placed their check on the table and Janet turned it over, tried not to gasp at the amount. She made a show of digging through her purse. She'd eaten exactly five bites of a meal that cost over thirty dollars, and it wasn't half as good as the spaghetti she made at home.

"Don't you dare," Grace said. "I got this."

Janet put her hands up. "Hey, just this once."

Grace winked at her and laid a hundred dollar bill on the table.

Janet walked back to the office, giving herself time to think things over and cool off. This wasn't the end of the world. She'd stay in touch with Grace and find a way to help spend some of that money. Maybe a business proposition where Grace would provide start up funds in return for a share of the profits. She knew someone who could cook the books and Grace would never know the difference.

How could one woman be so damn lucky? A fine looking man, a beautiful apartment, and now this. Life was unfair.

CHAPTER 6

Halfway down the block Janet stopped in a bookstore, deciding she could take a few extra minutes for lunch without getting fired, since Cheryl wouldn't want to lose two employees in the same day. She made a beeline for the business section and found an easy guide to writing business plans. She'd create a proposal Grace couldn't turn down—maybe something to do with fashion or interior design. An upscale boutique might do the trick.

Janet hurried out of the store, now truly late, and spotted Dajour leaving a restaurant across the street. An attractive woman clung to his arm, laughing at something he'd said. Janet couldn't resist this opportunity. Trotting across the street at an angle that would bring her in front of them, she positioned herself on the sidewalk and pretended to search for something in her bag.

She looked up suddenly. "Well, hi there! How are you, Dajour? I didn't expect to run into you today."

He stopped in front of her, looking uncomfortable. "Hey, Janet, what's up."

"Oh, nothing much. I just finished having lunch with your girlfriend—Grace." She focused on the woman beside him, a young hussy in a tight suit. The skirt ended halfway up her thighs, revealing plenty of leg. Janet looked the woman up and down, raised her eyebrows, and then met Dajour's gaze. He didn't offer to introduce her.

"Well, it was nice running into you two, but I've gotta run before I'm late for work."

"That's cool," Dajour said. "I'll tell Grace I ran into you."

Sure you will, honey. Janet flashed him a phony smile and said under her breath, "And she ain't gonna like what I got to tell her."

"Huh?" Dajour frowned.

Janet waved at him. "Nothing! Bye, have a good one."

"Shit!" Dajour pulled Roxanne forward and they started walking again. "I did not need to see her."

"Who was that?" Roxanne asked, hanging back to watch Janet disappear around the corner.

"She works with Grace and they're sort of friends, but Grace doesn't trust her. She likes to flirt with me, which doesn't set well with Grace."

"I can understand that," Roxanne said.

"Man, I know she's gonna tell Grace she saw us."

"Maybe she won't. A lot of women choose to mind their own business, contrary to popular belief."

Dajour spotted his truck ahead and pulled out his key chain. "Knowing Janet, she'll do whatever will cause the most trouble." He unlock the doors and opened the passenger side door for Roxanne, helping her climb into the truck. "You're sure you don't mind riding in this old thing?"

"Of course not. I think trucks are sexy."

Dajour climbed inside and started the engine, which always needed an extra goose on the accelerator. "Maybe I do need a new truck," he muttered.

Roxanne rolled down her window, since the air conditioning wasn't working. "I don't know, Dajour. Maybe you should come right out and tell Grace about everything."

"What makes you say that?" He glanced at her, surprised.

"I wouldn't want there to be any fallout between you two because you're keeping things from her."

He maneuvered around a slow moving garbage truck and slipped into the left hand lane, causing a taxi driver to lean on his horn. Dajour gave him the finger and kept driving. "I really want this engagement thing to be a surprise. If she asks me anything about you, I'll make up some story. Besides, she trusts me and she knows I wouldn't cheat on her. And she oughta know enough not to believe Janet."

"And just how does she know that?"

He smiled at her.

"And what does that mean? Did Janet do more than flirt with you? Come on—I wanna hear all the dirt."

"We were at the office Christmas party last winter—a real stuffy affair in a fancy restaurant. I was in the foyer outside the bathroom trying to make a phone call, and here comes Janet all by herself—drunk. That woman guzzles white wine like water." Dajour checked the side mirror and swung the truck back into the other lane. "She definitely made a pass at me. In fact, I had to duck into the men's room to get away from her."

"Did you tell Grace?" Roxanne asked.

"Nope. I handled it myself, and I sure didn't want to stir up trouble and give Grace an excuse to quit her job. But I think she suspected something."

"Yeah, us women have an instinct for that kinda thing."

"Well, the point is, I guess Janet knows better than to try and pin something on me."

"Let's hope so," Roxanne said.

Janet rushed back to work, barely conscious of where she was going. Seeing Dajour with that woman was a sign—she knew it. There had to a way she could use this to her advantage. She'd take a few days to sort things out and come up with a plan.

She was surprised to find Grace loading stuff from her desk into a cardboard box. Cheryl wasn't around, so Janet relaxed in Grace's cube and watched her pack.

"We're gonna miss you, girl."

"Will you put in for my job?" Grace asked, placing a photo of her parents in the box.

Janet shrugged. "I might. Thanks for lunch today."

"Any time." Grace held up a picture of her and Dajour on vacation. They stood in front of a lake and Dajour's arm was draped over her shoulder. Grace displayed a tiny fish about three inches long—the catch of the day. She smiled and showed Janet the photo. "I love this picture. Remember that camping trip I told you about?"

"How's everything going between you and Dajour?" Janet asked.

Grace smiled. "Pretty good. Better than ever, as a matter of fact. We're buying a house together and he'll be starting his own business before long. Things are definitely looking up." She shut down her computer. "All my files are up to date and you know my system. If you have any questions, just call me at home."

Janet sat in the chair beside the desk and crossed her legs. "I'm glad to hear things are going well. You aren't just saying that are you? I mean, you can tell me anything—we're friends."

Grace frowned. "Yeah, I mean exactly what I said. Why?"

"Oh, no reason. I was just asking, that's all."

Grace continued staring at her.

"I mean, I've heard winning the lottery can be stressful—in a good way—but it puts a strain on relationships. Geraldo did a show about it. Or maybe it was Oprah."

"Uh huh." Grace emptied out the middle drawer of her desk, dumping half the stuff directly into the trash can.

"Hey, I'll take that." Janet grabbed a hand mirror before it disappeared and used it to check her lipstick. "Trust is very important in a relationship, and I'm glad you two have that."

Grace closed the flaps on the box, grabbed her car keys, and snapped off the light. "Ready to go? This office is officially closed."

"How many people do you trust?" Janet followed Grace out of the room.

Grace paused. "Not too many, maybe two or three. You're one of them. Then there's Mama and Daddy, and my man."

They reached the front of the office suite and Janet opened the double doors for Grace, who turned to look back for a moment before leaving. "I'd like to say I'm gonna miss this place, but that would be a flat out lie."

"I'm glad to see you're cautious of the people you deal with," Janet continued. "Friends and close associates are like apples, you know. Sometimes you think you know somebody and they turn out to be rotten to the core."

Janet pushed the elevator button and Grace gave her a funny look. "What's wrong, Janet? You're talking weird, with all this mumbo jumbo about rotten apples. You been watching the soaps again?"

"It's nothing. I'm just missing you already. Who's gonna fight with old Cheryl and keep us entertained?"

Grace laughed. "You'll just have to take over. And don't worry about me, 'cause I'm having the time of my life. Stay in touch and give me a call soon."

After Grace quit her job, life became even more hectic. Her wardrobe quickly outgrew the closet space, even though she gave away most of her old clothes. Boxes of new merchandise she couldn't unpack were stacked in the corner of the living room, and real estate brochures littered the kitchen table. They needed more space, and soon.

On Thursday evening she was talking on the phone and stirring a pot of spaghetti sauce on the stove when Dajour came home from work.

He kissed her on the cheek. "Honey, I brought somebody for dinner."

She hung up the phone and hugged him, loving the manly smell of sweat and wood shavings on his body. "That's fine, baby. I've got plenty of food here, but nothing fancy. Is this something to do with your new business? If it is, then maybe we'd better take him out to eat."

Dajour laughed and kissed the tip of her nose. "You might say he's in the construction field, but there's no need to impress him."

The mystery guest stayed in the living room with Dajour, so Grace set the dining room table with a white linen cloth, her new china, and a set of Limoge candlesticks she'd bought on impulse from an upscale antique store. The table looked elegant and Grace could hardly wait to see how their guest would react. She called, "Gentlemen, dinner is served."

Dajour entered first, followed by a thin white boy with greasy, shoulder length hair secured by a filthy rubber band. A sick looking goatee sprouted from his chin. He slunk into the room like a whipped puppy, staring at the floor. For a second Grace thought he might pee on the carpet.

Dajour clapped him on the back. "Grace, this is Billy Bodine from Louisiana. He works with me."

Grace accepted Billy's limp handshake, her mouth hanging open. "Hello, Billy. Glad you could join us for dinner." She gave Dajour the evil eye, but he just grinned back at her.

"Man, look at all that food. You didn't tell me this was a *par-tay!*" Billy ate half the spaghetti, inhaled the sauce, and polished off three quarters of the garlic bread before he came up for air. Conversation was limited to a few comments between Grace and Dajour—Billy was focused on eating everything in sight, and she doubted his conversational skills were up to it anyway.

After dinner, Dajour planted Billy in front of the TV and followed Grace into the kitchen where she was rinsing plates at the sink. Putting both arms around her from behind, he nuzzled her neck and whispered, "Thank you!"

She spun around. "You better thank me! Bringing that pitiful looking drug addict into our apartment. He and his friends will steal us blind, now they know where you live. And who knows what kind of diseases he's got. I'm gonna wash these dishes in boiling water."

"Now, slow down. I wouldn't bring a drug addict up here, you know that. He's been in rehab for six months—I checked it out before I hired him."

Grace dried her hands on a dishtowel. "So what's the point? He's NOT staying here no matter how nice you ask me." She tried to flip Dajour with the towel, but he caught it and pulled her close.

"I just want to help, give him a second chance. I found out he sleeps in the back seat of an abandoned car in an empty lot near the construction site. I'd like to find a room for him, pay the first month's rent, and get him some decent clothes to wear on the job. Plus he needs money for groceries."

"How about a razor so he can shave?" Grace asked. "And don't forget deodorant and toothpaste."

"All that stuff, plus a big bar of soap. This kid's got potential—I know it. He comes from a good background, believe it or not. I've talked to his counselor."

"So you need a check." Grace was already reaching for her purse.

"Isn't that what money's for—to help people?"

Grace pulled out her checkbook, wrote a five thousand dollar check, and handed it to Dajour. "You'd better help him open a bank account. This should get him started."

"Thanks, babe. I knew you'd understand." Dajour hugged her again. "I'll help you load the dishwasher, then get him hooked up with a room. You want to come with us?"

Grace pictured Billy's greasy butt in the back seat of her new Bentley. "Nah, I've got stuff to do here. You go on."

"Nice girlfriend you've got," Billy said. He rolled down the window of Dajour's truck and hung his arm outside.

"She's a good woman." Dajour agreed.

"So I heard she won the lottery or something." Billy glanced at him.

"Something like that." Dajour slowed the truck and leaned forward to check the street signs. He was taking Billy to a residential hotel that had clean rooms and cheap rates. He'd once stayed there for a few weeks himself when times were tough.

"Watch out for money, it'll screw up your life."

Dajour laughed. "Man, you sound like a philosopher. You ever had money?"

"Oh yeah. I grew up in a big ass mansion on Long Island, went to private boarding schools in Switzerland, the whole works. My dad's the CEO of a big company. I saw him maybe twice a year. My family's like totally screwed up. Sometimes I wish we were poor."

"Well, now you are," Dajour said. "Is it better?"

Billy braced one foot against the dashboard and tied his ragged tennis shoe. "Hey, it's real. This way I know who my friends are."

Dajour stopped in front of a three story brick building with a burned out neon sign dangling from one of the second floor windows. A printed sign read: The Stickles Hotel for MEN. CASH ONLY. He handed Billy fifty bucks. "This'll get you a room for the night, plus a good breakfast. Tomorrow after work we'll sit down and talk about your future."

"Thanks, man."

Dajour stayed put until Billy went inside, because he didn't want the kid sneaking off and using the money for drugs. When Billy didn't reappear after fifteen minutes he figured it was safe to leave.

Driving home, he pondered Billy's words. He'd hoped the lottery money wouldn't change their lives, but he could already see things would be different. The big question was—could he and Grace hold it together?

CHAPTER 7

Later that evening Dajour and Grace lay in bed, cuddling and watching the late news. Now that Grace didn't have a job she liked to stay up until after midnight, but Dajour still had to get up at six and insisted on getting to sleep by eleven. He pointed the remote, snapped off the TV, and reached for the light on his side of the bed.

"How's the construction company coming?" Grace asked.

"Just great. We'll finish this job in another few days and move on to the next."

"No, I mean *your* company. Are you making plans? Tomorrow I'm gonna open a bank account for you and deposit the money you'll need to get started. You'd better think about renting an office and hiring some people."

He yawned. "I'm thinking about it. I've already picked the guys I'll take with me when I quit. I'll need to buy equipment, get a license, furnish the office and hire a secretary—there's a lot to think about."

"But it's a good thing, right? Isn't this what you always dreamed about?"

He paused. "I'm excited, but maybe a little scared. If I was doing it on my own, I'd build the business gradually—you know, little jobs here and there, working my way up the ladder. Starting this big makes me wonder if I can handle it."

Grace snuggled against him. "Of course you can. You're the most organized person I've every met."

The telephone rang.

"Don't answer it," Grace said. "I don't feel like being bothered."

"It might be business." Dajour turned the light back on.

"Who's going to call you for business in the middle of the night?" Grace picked up the receiver. "Hello?" She held the phone out, staring at it. "They hung up on me."

Seconds later the phone rang again. "Come on now." Grace answered. "Hello?" She shouted into the receiver, "Hello! Hello!"

The telephone rang again and Dajour reached for it, but Grace snatched it up. "Whoever's playing on my God damn phone better quit! You think you can hide behind star six seven, but all I have to do is call the operator and have your fuckin' phone cut the hell off! You don't know who you're dealing with."

Grace heard the shrill voice of Miss Charletta, Dajour's widowed mother. "If I have to come up there to wash your mouth out with soap at eleven o'clock at night, so be it."

"Who is it?" Dajour asked.

Grace covered the receiver with her hand. "It's your Mama."

Dajour rolled over and shouted, "Damn! Hey, Mama!"

Miss Charletta snapped, "You tell that Dajour I heard what he said, and I'll come up there and wash his mouth out too."

Grace giggled. "I'm sorry Miss Charletta. I thought you were an obscene caller. Someone called two times before you and hung up on me."

"I don't care, Grace. That was just as unladylike as you could possibly get. That was probably me anyway. I'm trying to figure out how to use this new phone. Where are you anyway?"

"In bed," Grace told her.

"Is Dajour there with you?"

"Now, Miss Charlotta, you know we're both consenting adults and...."

"Well, is he?"

"Yes."

"Then put my son on the phone."

With relief Grace handed the phone to Dajour, and then scooted closer so she could catch both sides of the conversation. It wasn't difficult to hear Miss Charlotta's voice, even with the receiver plastered against Dajour's ear.

"Hello?" Dajour asked.

"Don't hello me! You know who this is."

Dajour scooted up higher on his pillows. "Hey, Mama."

"Don't you be making me a bunch of grandbabies over there when you haven't put a ring on that girl's finger. You know how I feel about that sort of thing."

Grace whispered "Right on, Mama."

Dajour laughed. "Don't worry about that. All of that'll come in good time."

"Uh huh. You put Grace back on the phone."

Dajour obediently passed her the phone, rolling his eyes. "Good luck," he whispered.

"I'm here," Grace said.

"I just wanted to say good night, baby, and remind you to answer the phone like you had some training next time. I know your Mama raised you better than that."

"Yes, she did, Miss Charlotta. Thank you for your concern."

"Good night and God bless."

Grace tossed the phone into a basket filled with clean laundry, laughing. "No offense, Dajour, but you have the world's nosiest Mama. How come you don't ever say anything to help me out when she starts talking a hole in my head?"

Dajour stretched his arms and yawned. "You're a big girl, Grace. You can handle one tiny little woman."

She snorted. "One tiny little woman with the disposition of a rattlesnake. At least I protect you from my Mama."

Dajour closed his eyes. "Good night, Grace. Will you please turn off the light?"

She switched off the lamp, and then stared at the ceiling, watching patterns of light cast by the street lights outside. "Dajour?"

"Yes." His voice sounded groggy.

"Let's play a game of Be Honest."

"Grace, I'm not playing Be Honest with you at—what time is it? He rolled over and checked the clock. "It's after eleven and I need sleep."

She sat up in bed. "Come on, Dajour, I ask one question and then you ask one. That's it, I promise."

He sighed and folded both hands behind his head. "Fine, you start."

"No, you go first."

"Okay, I'm going back to sleep. See you in the morning." He turned over on his side and faked a loud snore.

Grace shook him. "You're not going back to sleep until you play, Dajour."

"All right then. Here's my question: Why don't you ever listen to anything I say? Be honest."

Grace thought for a moment. "Because sometimes you remind me of the little man on my shoulder. Sometimes I just want to knock him off. My Mama always told me, 'Look before you leap,' and I didn't want to hear that advice. Guess I don't want to hear it from you either. Be honest."

"Your turn," Dajour said.

Grace rolled over onto her stomach. "Am I the sexiest woman you've ever been in love with? Be honest."

"No. Be honest."

Grace frowned. This wasn't what she expected to hear. "No? What do you mean, 'No?'" Be honest."

"You said only one question." Dajour grinned at her in the half light from the windows.

"I have another one, and you'd better let me ask it before you get into trouble."

"But it's my turn."

Grace rolled her eyes. "Fine. Ask me."

"Why'd you pick your nose at my aunt's house that day and wipe your finger on the wall like nobody saw you? Be honest."

Grace punched him in the arm. "Dajour, you know I did not do trifling shit like that. Be honest."

He laughed. "I'm just fucking with you. Now can I get some sleep?"

"No. Don't play with me. It's my turn and I wanna know—have you cheated on me since we've been living here? Be honest."

"That's really a stupid question. What do you mean since we've been living here? I've never cheated on you, Grace. Who told you...."

"It's okay, Dajour. Just answer my question."

"NO."

"Good." Grace fluffed her pillow and pulled the covers around her shoulders.

"Is that it?"

"Yes. Good night, Dajour." Grace turned over and closed her eyes, leaving Dajour to stare at the ceiling, wide awake and totally confused.

Janet worked like crazy putting together a business proposal for Grace. Instead of a dress shop she decided to open an antique store—mostly so she could travel around the country attending auctions and estate sales, which sounded glamorous. She found a store for rent in a good location, crunched the numbers, and hired an accountant to help with the final draft. When everything was in order, she invited Grace to lunch.

She selected a Mexican restaurant and called ahead for reservations, booking a quiet table near the front windows. The antique store located directly across from the restaurant fit right into her plans.

Janet arrived early, placed her folder on an empty chair, and checked her watch half a dozen times. The Mexican food smelled spicy and wonderful, but she knew the knot in her stomach wouldn't let her enjoy it. She mopped her forehead with a napkin and tried to stay calm.

Grace was fifteen minutes late, but at last Janet saw her cruise by in the silver Bentley, then park alongside the curb. People on the sidewalk stopped to watch Grace emerge from the car. She looked fabulous in a pink designer suit and big sunglasses. A couple of men rushed to hold the door as she entered the restaurant.

Janet waved, and the hostess led Grace to the table.

"Girl, you're wearing the hell out of that suit," Janet said. Her own dress was three years old and had survived a dozen trips to the dry cleaners.

"Thanks. I found it at Nieman Marcus last week. You should really shop there." She opened the menu. "I have an appointment to look at a house this afternoon, so I can't stay long. Hey, it's great to see you." She reached across the table and touched Janet's arm. "What's happening at the office?"

Janet passed on the latest gossip, including Cheryl's bad

hairdo. Grace ate nachos and glanced around the room to make sure everyone noticed her—or at least that's how it looked to Janet.

"So I did get your job, and that's great, but I want to do more than that with my life." Janet slid her folder across the table. "I have an idea that will make money for both of us. How'd you like to own part of an antique store—like that one?" Janet pointed to the shop across the street.

"Hmmm," Grace said. "You know I love antiques."

"So do I. And so do lots of other people. Anyone can furnish a home with new stuff, but people with *real* class buy antiques." She rushed on as Grace opened the folder. "I've found a store for rent in a great location and I had an accountant run the numbers for us. All I need is a little help getting started and this business will take off on its own."

Grace took her time reading the papers, raising her eyebrows when she reached the final figure. She cleared her throat.

"What do you think?" Janet clenched her hands beneath the table.

Grace sipped her water. "This has potential, it really does. Let me take it to my accountant, have a look at the store, and I'll get back to you."

Janet handed her a key. "I borrowed this from the owner so you can look around. I'll need it back in a couple of days."

"That's cool. I didn't know you had such a head for business."

"We'd make a great team, Grace. Two sisters. In fact that's what we could name the store—Two Sisters Antiques."

Grace laughed. "Or how about Two Antique Sisters? I like that. Now let's get down with some hot food."

Janet relaxed her shoulders and took a deep breath. Grace hadn't said yes, but she hadn't said no either.

The next morning Grace drove to her parents' house, armed with real estate brochures, her checkbook, and some phone numbers. She parked the Bentley behind Daddy's old truck and felt a pang of sadness when she realized the plates had expired. He'd never drive again. She remembered riding in that truck as a little girl when going to town with Daddy was a special treat. He'd take her out for ice cream once a month—just the two of them, and she felt so grown up when they walked into the drug store together and sat on stools at the soda fountain. She'd spend five minutes studying the menu, but she always ordered a chocolate cone with sprinkles.

Grace locked her car and walked around back to the kitchen door. This was no time for sentiment—she needed to be strong. Half an hour later, she'd lured Mama into the kitchen for a private talk.

"I found the perfect house for you and Daddy. It's got handicap access inside and out, a heated swimming pool, and a hot tub for your arthritis. I'll pay for a housekeeper and gardener. We can even hire a private nurse when the time comes."

Mama looked through the pictures and then placed them back on the table, shaking her head. "Baby, I appreciate this, I really do. But we don't want to move. If I put your daddy in a strange house he'd never figure out where he was. And if he was in his right mind he'd never forgive me. We worked hard to buy this place, and we love it here."

"But Mama, the neighborhood...."

"This is *home,* Baby. We belong here."

Grace sighed and pushed the pictures aside. "All right, but I'm leaving these here in case you change your mind."

Mama carried the pictures over to the counter and added them to a pile of papers where they'd never see daylight again.

"More coffee, sweetheart?" she hovered over Grace with the pot.

Grace held out her cup for a refill. She still had business with Mama. "Now then, I talked to a home nursing service and hired a woman who'll come in during the day. She'll help get Daddy dressed, clean the house, do laundry—anything you need. And it's all paid for, so don't worry about a thing."

"Now, Grace, I don't want a strange woman coming in here. We're doing just fine."

"Mama, look at you! You haven't washed your hair in days, your clothes are a mess, you've lost weight. I'm so worried."

"The best thing you can do is come by and visit whenever you can. Seeing you is like a tonic for both of us."

"Can I take you shopping, Mama?" Grace asked hopefully.

"Child, I don't need more clothes. Where'm I gonna wear them? You know, money ain't everything in life and it won't bring happiness."

"Well, I've never had this much fun. I'm happy."

"Just don't let it change you." Mama patted her on the cheek. "Stay just as sweet as you are. Why don't you go relax and watch TV with your Daddy while I fix us something to eat?"

Daddy was in the den watching cartoons, and he barely noticed her. She sat beside him on the couch and took his hand. He used to work the New York Times crossword puzzles. Now it was Bugs Bunny and Mickey Mouse. After awhile, Grace wandered into her old room and lay down on the bed. Mama hadn't changed the flowered bedspread and matching curtains since she left home. The walls were the same pale pink, and a pile of stuffed animals covered half the bed. Her awards, certificates, and school pictures hung on the walls exactly as she'd left them when she went away to college. The whole room was like a shrine to her childhood.

Mama served ham for supper with collard greens, corn, rolls, macaroni and cheese, and scalloped potatoes. Grace ate until her stomach hurt, and there was still enough food left to feed half the families on the block. She tried to help with the dishes, but Mama pushed her out the door, saying, "Why don't you take Daddy for a walk. He'd love that."

So Grace and Daddy strolled around the block just like old times, and he whistled for her—a tune she remembered from childhood. Before dark she kissed them both good bye and hurried back to the city in her new car, thinking she really hadn't accomplished much.

CHAPTER 8

Three months later

Dajour unrolled a set of blueprints on his desk and switched on a lamp so he could see them better. Bidding for jobs was the most crucial part of owning a construction business, and he had a talent for it. He'd won a couple of contracts with the city by underbidding the competition—but now he had to consider bad weather, taxes, finding workers, buying quality materials at the lowest price, and a dozen other problems. No more going to work at seven and coming home at five with nothing to worry about. He'd never worked so hard in his life, but he loved every minute of it.

The secretary buzzed his office. "Mr. Wright, Roxanne is here to see you."

"Send her in," Dajour said.

Roxanne marched in and spun around on her toes to see the entire office. "Hey, I like what you've done with this old place."

"It's coming along. Grace decorated, naturally."

"Of course." Roxanne sat opposite him. "Everything's set up. All you have to do is pop the question."

Dajour winced. "Roxanne, I'm a little nervous about this. I think I might be having second thoughts."

"What? No you're not! Not after all the work I did to get you ready for this."

He walked over to the water cooler and filled a paper cup with water. "Want some?"

"No thanks. You haven't changed a bit."

Dajour returned to his desk, picked up a pencil, and began tapping on the blotter.

Roxanne stared at him through half closed eyes. "And to think I was starting to envy her."

Dajour tossed the pencil aside. "Her name is Grace."

"Well then, what's the problem?"

He shrugged, but didn't answer.

"Well?"

"It's no secret about the money...everyone knows."

"That's right. And?"

"I'm starting to think the money's changing her. She's not the same anymore; her judgement, her patience, even her basic common sense just seems to be gone."

"Like what? Give me an example."

"We went to a fancy restaurant a few days ago and she just flipped out for no reason. I think she wanted a lemon in her water. She actually threw the glass at our waiter—nearly hit him in the head. They almost asked us to leave and I've never been so embarrassed in my life."

"Wow, that's not good. Like a spoiled brat, right?" Roxanne looked at Grace's picture again. "She looks so nice."

"She is nice—she *was* nice. I don't know, maybe I'm tripping, but she just makes me nervous now. I don't know what she's gonna do next."

"Dajour, from what I hear, Grace has always been a little headstrong. She's cool, but she's impressionable."

"I think the money's beginning to change her."

Roxanne waved her hands in front of his face. "Dajour, wake up! Money doesn't change people.

"What? Yes it does. Look at Michael Jackson, Denis Rodman, and Latoya. Look at Latoya, Roxanne."

"I argue that money doesn't change people. Grace has always been like this and now she's reacting to a situation she's never been in. Personally, I think this crazy stage will blow over."

Dajour leaned back in his chair and stared at the ceiling. "I love her, Roxanne."

"I know. Just talk to her, tell her how you feel. Take her away from all of this. Since you've been together you've always been the level headed one."

"I guess. Yeah, you're right." He took a deep breath. "Are you going to help me pick out the ring?"

She got up, gave him a hug, and kissed him on the forehead. "That's better. Of course I'll help you."

He rummaged in his desk drawer and brought out a checkbook. "I almost forgot to pay you. I make the check out to Roxanne Richards, right?"

"Yep."

He scribbled on a check and handed it to her. "There you go—twenty grand. That's a pretty good price for planning a ninety thousand dollar wedding."

"Damn good." She kissed the check and grinned at him, then tucked it carefully inside her purse. "This goes straight to the bank."

Dajour walked her to the door and held it open. She turned and offered her hand. "It's a pleasure doing business with you."

Grace had never been so busy. Besides her regularly scheduled manicures, facials, pedicures, massages, yoga lessons, riding lessons, and sessions with a golf pro, she was starting an interior decorating business and helping Dajour with his company.

Shopping for the perfect house proved more complicated than she'd expected. Dajour was reluctant to leave the city, and he didn't want a formal home.

"I need to feel comfortable in my own house," he told her. "Find someplace where we can take our shoes off and relax in the evenings."

Finally they settled on a lovely estate called Heathfield, with a French country home built in 1872. The house had six fireplaces, beamed ceilings, beveled glass windows, hardwood floors, and French windows opening to brick terraces. The grounds featured a huge swimming pool, a tennis court, and a landscaped garden and woods. They both agreed it was perfect, although Dajour would have an hour's commute to the city. To solve that problem, Grace bought a luxurious condo near his office so they could stay over some nights.

She had her parents stay over for a weekend, but it didn't work out as she'd hoped. Daddy was totally confused in the big house and Mama didn't seem comfortable. On Sunday morning Daddy wandered off while she and Mama cooked breakfast. Panicked, they searched the grounds for half an hour and found him wading in the creek with his shoes on. She and Dajour took them home early.

"Well, that didn't go too well," Grace said as they drove back home. "I thought Mama would be happy for us, but she didn't seem to like our new house at all."

"It isn't that, Booby I think she's overwhelmed. No one expected us to own an estate."

"Well, I'd like to see her and Daddy in a good place where they'll be safe."

"Baby, you can't control them—they're happy where they are. Let it rest." Dajour took her hand. "How about a hot fudge Sunday?"

During the next week Grace selected furniture for both of their homes—antiques for the estate and modern for the condo. The best of both worlds. She'd almost forgotten about the antique store idea when Janet called and invited her to lunch again. "Give me a couple of days," she said. "My accountant still has the paperwork." Of course that was a lie, but it gave her time to do the homework. On a Friday afternoon she invited Janet up to the condo.

When Janet arrived, Grace was examining fabric swatches with a woman from the drapery shop. Two men from the carpet store crawled around the floor with tape measures, and several workers were hanging new cabinets in the kitchen.

"Sorry for the chaos." Grace led Janet into a room filled with furniture swathed in plastic covers. "I decided to redecorate before we move in—then I can use the condo to showcase the interior design business, and get a tax deduction." She swept the cover off a gorgeous leather chair. "If you'll wait right here, I'll get us something to drink from the kitchen."

Grace grabbed two bottles of water from the refrigerator and returned to Janet. She whipped the covers off another chair, seated herself, and uncapped her water. "Here's to decorating!"

Janet held up her bottle and they sipped French spring water.

"Now, about your proposal." Grace opened the folder she'd received from Janet. "My accountant was impressed with what you've done, but we have one question—do you really know much about antiques?"

Janet shrugged. "Not a lot. But I can learn."

"That's what I thought. In today's business climate if you don't know what you're doing it's almost impossible to succeed. And buying antiques for resale can be risky."

"But I can pull it off," Janet said. "I'll work twenty four hours a day if I have to. I'll do anything to get out of that legal sweatshop."

Grace recognized the desperation in Janet's voice and remembered how she'd felt a few months earlier. She softened her tone. "My accountant thinks we should find a different business, something more secure. Like dry cleaning."

Janet shook her head.

"How about a laundromat with a coffee bar?"

"Please!" Janet wrinkled her nose.

Grace consulted her list again. "Okay, maybe a day care center—those are big right now."

"I hate kids," Janet said.

"Well think of something you're good at, Janet. Otherwise it's a waste of money." They sat in silence for a few minutes. Grace had a million things to do and resented wasting time, but she tried to be pleasant. "Maybe you need to think this over for a few days and get back to me.""

"Wait, I've got it! How about a dating service for professionals? One where the clients make videotapes."

"Now there's an idea," Grace said. "You do know the dating scene and I haven't heard of anything like that in town. All we need is office space, video equipment, and a lot of marketing. Do the research and write it up for me."

Janet looked relieved. "Girlfriend, I'll have it ready by Monday or Tuesday. We're gonna take this town by storm."

As Grace led Janet to the door, she noticed her rundown shoes and a spot on the back of her dress. "Girl, you're gonna need a make over if we do this business, because you've got to look the part. Budget five thousand dollars for your wardrobe."

"I can get down with that." Janet grinned at her.

It was around that time the dreams started.

Grace sat behind a school desk in the front row of a classroom, wearing a plaid jumper with a white blouse and knee socks. She raised her head from the desk and watched a stern looking woman in a business suit write on a blackboard. Grace looked down at her clothing, bewildered, but now the woman was speaking.

"Less than a year before you fall from...grace."

"Huh?" Grace looked around the room, but the other children's faces were blank.

A clock ticked in the background, growing louder. The woman continued, "We want it all, we'll have it all, and you'll be dismissed."

The door opened with a loud creaking sound. Grace rose from her seat and crossed the room, standing with her back against the wall.

"We want it all, we'll have it all, and you'll be dismissed," said the teacher.

Terrified, Grace clung to the wall and sidled toward the door one step at a time. Just as she reached the opening the woman's face changed into a coiled serpent. A long reptilian tongue snapped out of her mouth and reached for Grace.

Grace screamed. A shadow passed outside the classroom door and Grace leaped into the hallway. For a moment she felt relief, until she realized the hall was empty and seemed to stretch on forever.

"Excuse me?" Her words echoed down the hall. She covered her mouth with one hand, realizing it might be best to stay quiet. The shadow appeared again, and then faded away at the end of the hall. Grace walked in the other direction toward what she hoped would be a door to the outside. Her shoes squeaked on the polished marble floor as she passed classroom doors, all closed, with shadowy figures inside. She didn't belong in any of these rooms. Where was her homeroom?

The ticking sound followed her, growing louder until it filled her head. She turned a corner and in the distance saw the old woman from the deli, wearing a long flowing dress and a scarf on her head. Grace picked up the pace until her calves ached, but the woman effortlessly stayed ahead of her.

"Ma'am? Ma'am? Where's the nearest exit?"

The woman paused and turned around. Grace slowed to a walk and approached with caution, afraid to look. When she glanced up, the woman's face was shadowed. Feeling safer, she moved close.

"Can you help me? I need to go home."

The woman extended a hand and Grace reached for it. Just as their fingers touched, Grace saw her face—a mass of squirming snakes in the shape of a woman covered by a cloak.

Grace screamed again and again, rooted to the spot by fear. The snakes broke apart and slithered to the floor, coiling around her feet. Finally she broke through her terror and turned to run. As she took the first step, Grace slipped into an abyss. She tumbled downward through black infinity.

She hit something and felt arms wrap around her body, holding her down.

"Grace! Wake up!" She opened her eyes, flailing both arms to fight off the snakes. Dajour had pinned her to the bed. "Hey, you're gonna give me a black eye. Calm down, baby."

She settled against the pillow, relieved to see Dajour's green eyes inches away. Her cheeks were wet with tears. She gave one last shuddering sob and buried her face against his chest.

"Bad dream?"

"Horrible! Snakes, evil women, a dark pit—I almost

died." She shuddered, trying to remember the woman's face. Before the snakes—had it been someone she recognized?

He rubbed her back. "I won't let anything get you. Snuggle up here beside me and we'll go back to sleep."

The next morning, Grace drove to Mama's house for breakfast. She sat at the kitchen table with an untouched plate of food in front of her.

"So what does it mean?"

Mama poured a cup of pancake batter into the old cast iron skillet she'd used since she and Daddy were married. "You need prayer."

"Besides that, Ma."

"Sounds like someone's trying to put a root on you."

Grace rolled her eyes toward the ceiling. "Mama, please! Next you'll be talking about voodoo dolls and sacrificing chickens.

"Well, just look at how you've been acting lately."

"And how's that?" Grace found the pancake syrup in the cabinet, poured some in a saucepan, and put it on the stove to heat. Mama didn't believe in microwave ovens.

"When was the last time you went to church?"

Grace returned to the table and ran her fingers through her hair. "Please! Why do you have to turn everything into a damn prayer meeting?"

Mama pointed the spatula at her. "Uh huh. That's what I'm talking about. You better be glad I'm convinced someone put a root on you, because if I wasn't...." She picked up a smaller skillet and held it aloft. "This skillet would be right upside your apple head."

Grace put her head in her hands. "So what do I do now? I can't stand another dream like that. I feel like somebody punched me in the stomach."

"You know what to do. Get some holy water from Pastor Milloy, sit the holy water under your bed for a week, and after the week is through you pray over it. Then sprinkle it on your sheets."

"That is not the way to deal with problems, Ma. I probably need to see a psychiatrist, maybe get some Prozac or something. "

Mama shrugged and flipped the pancake. "Your daddy's mother tried to use a root on me, and it worked."

Grace picked at her food, half listening.

"The only way it won't work is if you continue to stay in that negative frame of mind and keep holding on to that chip you've been carrying around on your shoulder."

Janet waited in the beauty shop having her hair unbraided while thumbing through an old copy of Essence magazine.

She met Grace at the condo the day before and found herself in limbo *again* while Grace yammered with someone on the phone about whether to buy a crystal chandelier for the dining room or go with something modern.

On this visit Grace's living room was furnished with leather furniture in pale yellow with green and blue throw pillows. Stacks of boxes along the walls had yet to be unpacked. At least four different pedestals held sculpture and ceramic vases—some of which were cracked. Janet assumed the movers had broken them during delivery.

"I'm ready." Grace had finally joined her.

"You've got it looking great," Janet said. "How many bedrooms?"

"Just two. The master bedroom's not finished, but you're welcome to see it."

She followed Grace down the hall to a room with a huge picture window overlooking the city. A king-sized platform

Peter maly bed sat in the middle of the room and Janet pictured Dajour lying on it, waiting for her. She shook her head.

"Something wrong?" Grace asked.

"Oh, no. Just a headache."

Back in the living room she gave Grace the folder and waited for the verdict.

This time Grace smiled. "Hey, this is fine. I like it. Are you ready to get started?"

Janet heaved a massive sigh of relief. Finally the sleepless nights had paid off. She watched Grace write a check—this one much bigger than ten thousand dollars.

"Get yourself some clothes, rent the office, and start working on the marketing plan. We'll need TV and radio ads, a good slogan, a logo—you know the drill." Grace paced the floor. "Let me know as soon as you sign the lease so I can choose furniture. For now we'll need to meet once a week to talk things over and make plans."

Janet took notes and left the apartment with a list of things to do. But first, she'd quit her job and tell Cheryl where to get off.

"Sit up straight, honey."

Janet realized she was sinking in the chair. Shantelle adjusted the cape and continued loosening the tight braids. "So what's the latest with Grace? She spend all that money yet?"

"She's working on it." Janet knew better than to gossip in the beauty shop, because every word she said would go right back to Grace. There was plenty she wanted to say, like how Grace had started treating her like hired help instead of a friend. Like the ten thousand dollar check, which still rankled.

"How you want this hair?" Shantelle asked.

"Sophisticated," Janet said. "Make me look better than Grace."

Grace knocked on Pastor Milloy's front door. She could see him through the window, pacing the floor in his study and talking to himself—most likely practicing his sermon. She'd endured those mind numbing sermons for years until she graduated from high school and moved away from Mama's influence.

He opened the door, blinking in the sunlight. "Grace Johnson! What a surprise. Come inside." He led her into the study and motioned to a chair.

Grace seated herself and looked around. Nothing had changed since she'd last been here ten years ago before her sister's wedding. The same pictures of Jesus on the wall, a Bible on his desk, framed certificates on the shelves. But the pastor himself seemed older, more worn.

He pumped her hand. "Grace, I am so happy to see you. It's been such a long time. How many years has it been?"

"I've been busy I guess. I don't get back to visit like I used to."

"You shouldn't ever be too busy for the Lord, Grace."

"I know." She squirmed in the chair. "I appreciate all you do for Mama and Daddy. I don't know how they'd get by without the church."

"They've done a lot for us over the years. Everybody just loves them to death, and they still come to church every Sunday no matter what." He gave her a pointed stare.

"I belong to a church in the city," Grace said. She didn't mention that she only attended on Easter Sunday and Christmas and had to drag Dajour kicking and screaming through the doors.

Pastor Milloy sat behind his desk. "Well, what can I do for you?"

"I need holy water, Pastor."

"Any particular reason why?"

"I've been surrounded by bad energy lately."

"You don't need holy water, Grace. You need to remove yourself from the negativity and surround yourself with the Lord."

"Well, can I have some holy water in the meantime?"

Pastor Milloy laughed and shook his head. "You always did have a ready answer." He opened a drawer, took out a small bottle, and handed it to Grace. "Be careful—it's powerful stuff."

Grace held the bottle in her hand. She felt better already. "Thanks so much, Pastor. I'll see you one Sunday soon."

As she went down the porch steps he called after her, "I hope you find whatever it is you're looking for, Grace,"

She smiled. "Me too."

Across the street from Reverend Malloy's house Grace recognized the back side of Maple Park, where she'd played as a child. Most of the space was now a baseball diamond, but the town fathers had left one corner intact. Huge maple trees shaded a stone BBQ grill, and that old fashioned swing set was probably the same one she remembered.

Without really thinking about it, Grace found herself crossing the street. She and her best friend Tasha used to bring their dolls to the park for cookouts. They'd deck themselves out in Mama's cast off dresses, accessorized with high heels, fake pearls, and straw hats. They usually packed their dolls inside an old baby buggy and sometimes added the family cat—when they could catch him.

Grace slipped off her shoes, letting the grass tickle her feet. On impulse she stretched on her back under one of the trees and stared into the leafy branches. A robin landed above her with a worm in its beak. Children shouted in the distance.

A light breeze ruffled the pale green leaves. Before long she closed her eyes and drifted off.

Something awakened her—a presence more than a sound. She opened her eyes and saw a young girl with ebony skin sitting cross legged on the grass, watching her with a solemn expression. The girl wore white patent leather shoes, pink socks with ruffles, and a matching pink dress. Her hair was tied in braids that ended with pink and white ribbons. She held a doll on her lap.

"Hello there," Grace said.

"Hello." The girl's brown eyes never left her face.

"You're all dressed up. Are you going somewhere special?"

The girl pointed to a small brown suitcase under the swing set. "My name's Francine and I'm running away."

"My goodness. Are you old enough to run away?"

"I'm six and a half. That's old enough."

Grace wondered what to say next. She looked around, but didn't see anyone else in the park besides a few boys playing baseball. Shouldn't someone be looking for this child? "Where do you live, Francine?"

"Over there a ways, in a yellow house." Francine pointed across the street.

Grace didn't see any yellow houses. "I bet your Mama's worried about you. How come you're running away?"

"Because she whipped me." A tear slid down her cheek and she sniffed.

Grace found a tissue in her pocket, leaned forward, and wiped away the tear. "Did you do something wrong?"

"I'm always running into the street 'cause I forget to stop and look for cars. Mama said she spanked me so I'll remember next time."

"You know, I had the same problem," Grace said. "I never stopped to think before I did things. One time I jumped into the deep end of a swimming pool and almost drowned."

"Did it hurt?" Francine's eyes grew wide.

"No, and I wasn't even scared. I guess I didn't learn much from it, because I just kept on running into things."

"Maybe you should stop and think. That's what Daddy tells me—stop, look, and listen." Francine looked at the doll on her lap—a faded Raggedy Ann. "I left my doll out in the rain and she got wet."

"I used to have a doll just like that," Grace said. "I lost her somewhere."

Francine held out the doll. "You can have this one. I don't need her."

Grace smoothed the doll's red yarn hair and admired the black button eyes. "She's beautiful. Thank you, Francine. This means a lot to me. Maybe you'll show me where you live and I can meet your mother. Would that be okay?"

Francine nodded.

"Honey, I need to use the bathroom over there before we go. Will you wait for me right here?"

"Yes ma'am, I'll try."

Grace hurried to the bathroom—a concrete building in the center of the park that hadn't changed since she was a child. No toilet paper of course, but luckily she carried tissues in her purse. She combed her hair and straightened her clothing so she'd make a good impression on Francine's parents, who were probably worried sick about their daughter. She stepped outside and looked around.

The park was empty. Grace ran to the cookout area, shouting for Francine, but the child had disappeared along with her suitcase. One of the swings moved back and forth as though someone had just pushed it.

"Francine? Are you hiding?" Grace searched behind every tree and bush, hoping this was a childish game. When she returned, Raggedy Ann was sitting on the swing.

Clutching the doll, Grace crossed the street and knocked on Reverend Malloy's door.

"Grace! Do you need something else?" He looked surprised to see her and she suspected he'd been napping.

"Is there a little girl named Francine in the neighborhood?"

He scratched his head and leaned against the door frame. "Not that I can think of, and I know all the kids—unless she's visiting someone."

"Well, how about a yellow house?"

"Not now, but that blue house at the end of the block used to be yellow. In fact, they had a daughter named Francine, but that was years ago—before your time."

"Well, thanks anyway." Grace turned to leave, but the Reverend kept talking.

"...I'll never forget that day, a Sunday morning. Francine was dressed for church, waiting in the front yard for her Mama. Her brother threw a ball into the street and she ran after it, right in front of the church bus. Killed her instantly." He blinked hard. "The driver never forgave himself, though it wasn't his fault. Her family moved away after that and we never heard from them again."

Still clutching Raggedy Ann, Grace walked the two blocks to her parent's house, feeling dazed. Was it all a dream? If so, then where did the doll come from? She'd never heard of a haunted park, but just maybe....

She wanted to tell Mama what happened, but something stopped her. Hearing she'd seen a ghost would only confirm Mama's worst fears. She didn't mention the incident to Dajour because he scoffed at the supernatural—he'd say she'd fallen asleep, had a strange dream, and found the doll by accident.

Nevertheless, Francine stayed in her thoughts, and she vowed to find the little girl's grave the next time she was in town and leave some flowers. She placed Raggedy Ann among the pillows on her bed. She had a funny feeling those button eyes were trying to tell her something.

CHAPTER 9

G race divided the holy water in half—one vial for their bedroom in the condo and the second for their room at Heathfield. They'd sublet the old apartment to friends and sold most of the furniture, although Dajour insisted on keeping his favorite chair. Their new bedroom at the estate had bay windows overlooking the pool. Grace loved to relax on the king sized bed and watch the sheer white curtains flutter in the breeze.

Hearing the sound of a big truck outside the window, she got up and peeked outside to see what and who it could be. No one came up the long driveway by mistake. A big van from the furniture store had pulled up in front of the house. A couple of young men hopped out and started unloading furniture. Grace sighed. They really should use the delivery entrance, but it was too late now. She'd let the housekeeper handle things—that's why they paid the woman.

Grace did miss having close neighbors—somebody to drink coffee with, or at least talk to. People from the other estates were friendly when she met them in town or said hello at the mailbox, but they didn't socialize and usually just waved from their cars. Not once had anyone invited them over for drinks or dinner; but then again, neither had she. The neighbors were all white and most of the women stayed busy with charity events. Foxhunting seemed to be a major thing in Virginia society. Of course, she and Dajour had no clue how get started in that sport. She bought an expensive riding outfit and signed up for lessons at a local stable, but didn't really enjoy bouncing around on the back of a moving animal. Besides, she had a feeling people were laughing at her.

She returned to the bed and sorted through the mail on the bedside table. A pile of junk mail went directly into the wastebasket, along with several magazines she'd never read. She opened her own bank statement and then the statement for the joint account she'd opened for Dajour's business. Everything seemed in order until she spotted a check for twenty thousand dollars.

Frowning, Grace picked up the phone and dialed the bank. "Hello, this is Grace Johnson. I received my statement in the mail and I think there's been a mistake. Yes, my account number is 236739729. Check number 0156 is the one in question. Can you tell me who received it?"

She waited, drumming her fingers against the phone, and then listened for a few moments. "All right. Thank you. No, that'll be all."

Grace slammed the telephone down.

That evening she let the housekeeper go home early and fixed dinner herself, a roast with carrots and potatoes. At Heathfield they ate in a formal dining room instead of in the kitchen. In fact, the new kitchen had so many stainless steel appliances it seemed more like a restaurant.

Dajour seemed preoccupied, eating quickly and staring into space as he chewed.

Grace asked, "Any new projects going on with the business?"

He shook his head. "Nope. We're right in the middle of renovating those town houses in Georgetown and we just finished the Ainsley job. I'm working on a bid for a new shelter house at one of the city parks. Smitty's doing a great job as foreman and I've got Billy Bodine hanging drywall."

"So you have plenty of money in the checking account?" Grace refilled her water glass from a crystal decanter.

He glanced at her. "Sure. We even showed a profit last month. Why?"

"Oh, I just wondered. Your bank statement came today."

He swallowed a bite of roast. "That's good. Put it on my desk and I'll take it to the office in the morning."

Dajour didn't seem the least bit nervous about the bank statement, so Grace changed the subject. But that didn't mean she'd forget that twenty thousand dollar check.

The next afternoon Janet drove out to the estate to visit and talk about their business venture. Grace proudly showed her around, glad to have company. Sometimes she almost felt nostalgic about those cafeteria lunches back at the office. After the grand tour, they sat on the patio sipping tea from crystal glasses and eating French pastry.

Blooming iris, lilacs, and peonies scented the air and a gentle breeze ruffled their hair.

"This is the life," Janet said. "This is what I'm gonna have when the business takes off."

"Maybe you can move in next door, cause this neighborhood sure needs a little color. I've never seen so many stiff necked snobs in all my life." Grace fanned herself with a straw hat.

"Girl, you need to throw a big party, bring in a blues band and a couple dozen kegs."

"Maybe I'll just do that," Grace said. "It would serve 'em right." She was glad to see Janet finally had the fashion thing under control. She wore a crocheted tank dress with a scoop neckline and she'd gotten rid of those awful braids. With her hair short and shiny, Janet looked five years younger. "You look fine," Grace told her. "I like that dress."

"Neiman Marcus, like you said." Janet opened her attaché case and handed Grace a sheaf of papers. "I've rented the office and it's ready for your magic touch." She handed Grace a set of keys. "I've been thinking about names. How about Soul Mates, Romance Central, or 2 of a Kind?"

"Let's go with Soul Mates," Grace said. "We'll use soul music on the ads."

"Perfect." Janet sipped her tea and looked out over the grounds where a gardener was trimming rose bushes. "You have a pool boy?"

"Say what?"

"Aren't you supposed to hire a big healthy looking guy who wears a thong and hangs around the pool all day?"

Grace laughed. "Not yet, but if Dajour doesn't watch his back I may be doing just that."

They were silent for a minute, and then Janet said, "Grace, I feel like you've been avoiding me."

"Why do you feel like that? We see each other once a week."

Janet stirred her tea. "I don't know. We used to be so close and now we never talk about anything personal. It's like you don't want anything to do with me on a personal level."

Grace shifted her chair, moving out of the sun. "I've just been feeling strange lately. Nightmares and all."

"You don't seem happy."

"Well, I don't know if I am anymore."

Janet placed a hand on her knee. Grace let it stay there for a few seconds, then moved her leg away.

"You can talk to me about anything," Janet said.

Grace propped her feet on a chair and pulled her dress

up so her legs could get some sun. "I don't know if I can trust Dajour anymore."

"Oh, come on!"

"Lately he's so secretive and he's always gone. I know he's busy with the construction company and everything, but I feel like I'm being pushed further and further away from him. Him and everyone else, for that matter."

Janet looked around as though someone might be listening. "Well, I don't know about everyone else, but I'd definitely watch Dajour."

Grace tilted her head to one side. "Why'd you say that?"

Janet looked away. "Never mind. I really shouldn't have said anything. I need to mind my business."

"Janet, if you're really a friend you'll tell me, no matter what it is."

"Forget it. Let's talk about something else. Where'd you buy these plates?"

"JANET! If you don't tell me I'll kill you right now and have the gardener bury you under the hedge."

Janet held up her hands in submission. "Okay, okay. I think Dajour has been cheating on you."

Grace's jaw dropped. She hadn't really believed it, not deep down. And now here was the moment she'd dreaded. But now she *had* to know. "Keep talking."

"Well, do you remember the day when you first bought that car and we had lunch at a French restaurant? Bad food, slow service?"

"That could've been half the restaurants in town. But go on."

"Well, on my way back to the office I saw him with another woman, coming out of a restaurant. I watched them get into his truck and drive off together."

Grace lowered her head. "Why didn't you tell me as soon as you saw this, Janet? What were you thinking?"

"I didn't want to interfere. I didn't want to be wrong, and then you'd be miserable for nothing."

She looked up at Janet, whose eyes were sparkling. "So what now? What should I do?"

"Don't lose hope. Maybe it was something innocent. We don't know for sure he's cheating on you."

Grace blotted her eyes with a napkin. "I need to know for sure. I'll ask him about it tonight."

"Come on, Grace, pull it together. You think he'll tell the truth? You have to catch him in the act."

"And how should I do that? Drag him onto the Jerry Springer show and make him take a lie detector test?"

"No, crazy. Hire a detective."

Grace frowned, "Chile, please. That's so sleazy."

"No really, if you hire a good detective who knows what he's doing and get him to report back to you, then your problem is solved."

"Isn't that illegal or something? And how do I find a detective?"

Janet cleared her throat and did a little dance in her seat. "I used to date one." She opened her purse, pulled out a business card, and passed it to Grace. "Here you go."

"You used to date this guy, Janet?"

"Well, one date. But I was impressed with him."

Grace examined the card. It was expensive and professional looking—not a homemade job on somebody's computer. "So your telling me this man can find out if Dajour's cheating on me?"

"He'll tell you with evidence and pictures. Shit, he'll even be able to tell you what kind of tampons the bitch uses, if you want to know."

Grace took another sip of tea. "So when should I call him?"

"Anytime."

"Okay, I'll call him tomorrow while Dajour's at work." She sighed. "I just can't believe this is happening."

Janet guided her car through traffic on Route 95, her mind flooded with ideas. Owning a business with Grace was fine, but now it wasn't enough. By the time she parked in front of her building she had a plan. The first step was to reach Mason before Grace called him. She rushed into her apartment, found Mason's number in the bottom of her purse, and called his office. His secretary answered on the second ring.

Pacing the floor in front of the living room window, Janet told her, "I'm a friend of Mason's. I need to tell him about a job he won't want to miss."

"One moment please." Light jazz came on the line.

Janet carried the phone into the kitchen, poured a glass of wine, and wandered into the bedroom where she kicked off her shoes and settled against the pillows on her bed. She wasn't certain Mason would even recall her name, but he'd definitely be interested in what she had to say.

"Janet, I've been meaning to call you." His voice was liquid honey over the phone.

She stifled her impatience. He was a sexy man, but now she had more important things on her mind. "Yes, I'm sure you've been busy."

"I enjoyed our night together. Maybe we can get together soon."

"I'd like that Mason, but this is all about business. A friend of mine will be calling you and I expect to get something out of it."

He cleared his throat. "I don't give commissions."

"You will this time, because otherwise I'll tell her to call someone else. Her name is Grace and she just won 40 million dollars." Janet paused to let the words sink in. "Are you interested?"

"Very. So what'd you have in mind?"

"It should be a cakewalk—Grace thinks her boyfriend is cheating on her."

"Is he?"

"I'm not sure, but I know we can use this situation to our advantage if we work together. Are you in?"

"Baby, I'm with you all the way. This is better than sex."

Dajour parked his new Dodge Ram pickup outside a townhouse in historic Georgetown. He'd recently taken on a renovation job from another construction company that filed for bankruptcy. The insanely rich townhouse owners were nervous because they'd already flushed a bundle of money with the other company. Now Dajour spent at least an hour a day schmoozing with the wife, who kept making changes to the design plans. After two weeks he wished he'd never heard of these people.

The work site looked clean and efficient—the way he liked it. He found Smitty in the gutted living room squinting over a set of blueprints on the workbench.

"How's it going with those changes?" Dajour snapped on a work light hanging above the bench.

"Hey, boss." Smitty peeled off his Washington Redskins cap and swiped a handkerchief across his brow. His dark skin gleamed with sweat. "The electricians finished up this morning, so we started covering the walls on the top floor. That special paneling got here yesterday, thank you Jesus, but it's the ugliest stuff I've ever seen. Looks like somebody poured acid on it."

"That's how it's supposed to look—they paid extra to have it aged."

Smitty shook his head. "Don't make sense to me."

They climbed a staircase in the center of the house to the third floor. In the study a young guy with a pony tail hovered over a table saw. A window fan kept the sawdust stirred up, making it hard to breathe.

Smitty walked to the window and reset the fan to blow out instead of in. He shouted above the whine of the saw, "I've got Matt here, and Billy's hanging drywall in the master bedroom."

"How's he working out?" Dajour asked.

"He's slow, but I can't complain about his work."

"No problem, then. I'll have a look." Dajour stepped inside the room, which featured stained glass windows overlooking a shady backyard. The drywall looked good so far, but Billy had only managed to hang a few sheets. "Okay, so where is Billy?"

"Where has that fool kid got to? I just talked to him an hour ago." Smitty looked out the window as though he might see Billy in the yard. He went back into the study and made a cutting motion across his neck. Matt shut off the saw. "You seen Billy?" Smitty asked.

Matt shrugged and shook his head. "Not since noon. He said he felt sick and he looked like death warmed over."

"Arrrggggg." The sound came from a bathroom across the hall.

Dajour found Billy curled in a fetal position on the floor, alternately retching and clutching his belly. Dajour knelt and turned him over, shocked at the green tinge to his skin. He laid a hand on the boy's forehead. It felt hot.

"What's the matter?" Smitty asked.

"My stomach." Billy groaned and sat up to spit into the toilet. He propped himself against the wall, still curled up.

Dajour tried to straighten his legs, but Billy pulled away. "It hurts worse when I put my legs down. Just leave me alone and I'll be alright. I'll come back to work in a few minutes. Gotta hang drywall."

"Did you eat some bad food?" Dajour asked.

"I don't think so. I haven't ate nothin since last night."

"When did the pain start?"

"I've been hurtin for a couple of days, but it got real bad just a little while ago."

"Hold his legs down so I can see his belly," Dajour told Smitty. He explained to Billy, "I was a medic in the Navy and I need to check your stomach. I'm just gonna push on it a little bit." He pressed on the right lower quadrant.

"Ow! Boss, am I gonna die?"

"Not yet, Billy. I think you've just got a bad appendix. Smitty, you and Matt help me pick him up."

Dajour carried Billy downstairs in his arms—the kid only weighed about 130 pounds soaking wet. He loaded him in the truck and headed for the hospital.

Janet shifted in her chair. She needed to head back to the city before rush hour, but Grace just wouldn't shut up. They'd finished a pitcher of tea, along with the pastry, and her head buzzed from the caffeine-sugar high. She hated nothing worse than relationship stories. Who cared how somebody else met and what they said to each other? She was already sorry she'd told Grace about seeing Dajour with that woman. On the other hand, if Grace kicked him out of her life, it would be open season.

Grace waved her hands in the air. "You know, I can't believe I'm doing this. When Dajour and I first met, we just clicked. I mean with everything. Our views on life, relationships. On our very first date he told me I was a perfect one hundred percent. He said I didn't need to do a single thing for him to trust me completely.

Janet nodded, wishing for a cigarette. She'd stopped smoking months ago but at times like this she craved nicotine.

Grace took a breath. "He doesn't believe in the old 'I have to know you for six months to a year before I'll do something for you.' He let me hold his car after only three days of knowing me. He said if I was going to do him in, he'd rather find out in two or three weeks, not a year. And now after three—almost four—years I gotta go behind his back to see if he's cheating on me. Fate sure has a funny way of turning around and biting you on your ass every time."

"And that's just really unfortunate." Janet held her arm out, checked her watch, and feigned surprise. "Look at the time! I'd love to stay and chat, but I've got to get going."

"Where you got to go?" Grace asked.

"Everybody can't lounge around all day, Grace. I have work to do." She stood and gave Grace a hug. "Call me if you need anything. I'm sure this will all work out." One way our another, she thought.

They strolled to the front of the house where Janet had left her car, but obviously Grace didn't want to let her leave. When she started the engine Grace was still talking.

"Thanks for everything, Janet. I'm sorry about not hanging out like we used to, but we'll catch up one of these days."

Janet waved. "I'm gone."

"Bye."

When she looked back, Grace was standing in the driveway staring at the business card.

CHAPTER 10

The phone rang as Janet's car disappeared beneath the oaks lining the driveway. Grace ran back inside and grabbed it from the hall table.

"Honey, it's me. I'm gonna be late tonight. I had to take Billy Bodine to the hospital."

"What happened?" She carried the phone into the den and settled in one corner of the leather couch with both legs curled under her.

"Looks like appendicitis. We found him on the bathroom floor in the townhouse. Anyway, he doesn't have family here and they're taking him to surgery, so I'll hang around until it's over."

Grace wondered if Dajour was telling the truth, but this story sounded too crazy to be a lie. "Do you want me come and wait with you? I can bring takeout food."

"No, that's okay. Smitty's with me and we'll grab a bite in the hospital cafeteria. I should be home by nine."

That evening a hurricane blew up the coast, with high winds, thunder, and driving rain. Grace sealed all the windows in the house and closed the blinds, feeling a bit vulnerable. In the city she'd loved storms, but the open space on the estate gave her the creeps. Their big house with the brick turrets reminded her of horror movies where lightening flashed above the rooftops and unspeakable things hid in the basement. To make it worse, the telephones went out and the lights flashed on and off. She tried to read, but wind and rain battering the windows was too distracting. With all the trees on their property she couldn't even see the road or the neighbor's houses.

She started to take a shower, but changed her mind when she remembered the shower scene from *Psycho*. If Dajour walked in while she was in the shower she'd probably die of a heart attack. To work off nervous energy she turned on all the lights in the game room and played pool by herself.

Around eight thirty, she finally saw the headlights of Dajour's truck flash outside the front windows. Minutes later the garage door rumbled open.

He opened the back door and shouted, "Grace! Hey, Grace, you here?"

"I'm in here," she called from the game room.

Dajour appeared wearing only his boxers, drying his hair with a towel. "Hey babe, what's up?"

"Nice. What happened to you?"

"At the hospital I had to run through the storm to get my truck. It's really coming down out there."

"I noticed. How's Billy?" She took a shot for the 6 ball and missed.

"Good. The surgery went well, but his appendix had already ruptured. He's all hung up with IVs and stuff." He circled the table. "You playing pool?"

"Yup. Wanna play?"

"You can't beat me."

"Oh no?"

Dajour smiled. She tossed him a cue and then pulled a nickel from her pocket. "Heads or tails?" She flipped the coin.

"Heads."

Grace studied the coin, squinting. "It landed on tails. Rack 'em up."

"Aigh shawdy, that's cool."

"I know."

Dajour came up behind her and pulled her into an embrace. She turned, pressing herself against him. He kissed her. "Oh, you know, do you?"

"Uh huh." She kissed him back.

"What else do you know?"

"I know you wrote up a twenty thousand dollar check on that account of ours and didn't tell me about it."

He pulled back, frowning. "Oh, I forgot to...."

"Oh no, baby, don't worry about it. I was just wondering, because I remember back in the day when twenty grand was a lot of money, and now we can just pull it out of the bank like it's lunch money."

"Someone asked me to go half on an investment with them, so I did. I just forgot to mention it, that's all."

"Okay, so what are you waiting for? Rack 'em up!"

That night Grace stayed awake long after Dajour fell asleep. She watched him for awhile, loving the way he slept so soundly. Even the loud thunderclaps didn't disturb him. Would a guilty man be able to sleep like that, she wondered?

Her ex-boyfriend Troy had certainly slept well while he cheated on her for the last six months of their relationship. Several years before she met Dajour, Grace had lived with her first true love—Troy Summers. He was one hot looking man, full of life and energy, who loved partying at the clubs and hanging with friends. She found him irresistible, and so did a lot of other sisters. The man was so fine any woman would be proud to go home with him. It took her awhile to realize that underneath the surface charm, Troy was lazy, sneaky, and whorish. He promised to give up his other women when she moved into his apartment. Six months went by, and she began noticing things—perfume on his clothing, unexplained nights out, phone calls he took in the other room. He had a ready explanation for everything, but sometimes his stories sounded too good.

One night in bed Grace leaned on one elbow so she could look him in the eyes and asked straight out: "Troy, have you been sneaking around on me?"

He patted her on the cheek. "You know you're my woman. I don't need anybody else."

She wanted to believe him. She'd had a string of dead end relationship up to that point, so she crossed her fingers and hung in there with Troy. She kept herself looking good, spent a fortune on clothes, and cooked up a storm. The club scene got old after awhile, but she went along and tried to have a good time.

Everything was cool until Grace found a pair of panties in his gym bag and noticed quite a few of his Pure Playaz briefs started disappearing. Naturally, he had a story: the guys at the gym put women's underwear in his bag as a joke and his own underwear was in a locker at the gym. Grace only half believed him, but she wasn't ready to call it quits. Instead, she tried harder to please him.

A few weeks later she got an anonymous letter that said: "You're one stupid sister. Don't you know Troy's seeing another women on the side?" The writer thoughtfully provided an address and phone number. Grace cruised by the woman's house that evening and, sure enough, Troy's car sat in the driveway. She wanted to knock on the door and punch him out, but lost her nerve. Instead, she waited until he got home in the wee hours of the morning and confronted him. He lied. He pleaded. She gave him another chance.

But the next evening when she came home from work

he'd piled her stuff in the hallway and changed the locks on the apartment. Grace stayed with a friend for a few weeks and finally moved into the depressing studio apartment. She gained ten pounds and nearly lost her job for being absent minded. She sat by the phone waiting for it to ring, hoping Troy would miss her as much as she missed him. It took awhile, but by the time Dajour entered the picture, Grace figured she was over Troy and ready for another try.

Now, here she was, back at square one. Was Dajour cheating? If she asked him he'd deny it, just like Troy. Confrontation wasn't the answer. Now, with her money she had the means to check on him without waiting for the other shoe to drop.

She padded into the bathroom, closed the door so the light wouldn't disturb Dajour, and dug in the trash can for the business card she'd thrown away before they went to bed.

She leaned against the velvet cushions in the bay window, holding Raggedy Ann and watching the rain. What would it hurt to call the man and find out for certain? Maybe he'd tell her Dajour was faithful, which would put her mind at ease. On the other hand, if Dajour had another woman on the side, she'd claw the bitch's eyes out. Not really, but the thought made her feel better. He'd learn his lesson and they could go on from there.

Grace wanted to call someone, but it was 2 AM and even her own mother wouldn't appreciate being awakened in the middle of the night. Maybe she needed to spend more time with Dajour—drive into the city and have lunch with him a couple of times a week, show more interest in his work. She'd do whatever it took to hold onto him.

After Janet's call Mason had cancelled his one appointment for the afternoon and waited around the office, hoping Grace would get in touch. By five p.m. she still hadn't called, so he went home disappointed. However, the next morning he heard from her bright and early. His female clients usually fell into two categories: pissed off, or hopeful. Grace sounded like the second type. She still wasn't sure about her boyfriend and hoped for the best outcome. Instead of seeing her in the office, he offered to drive to her estate, hoping the visit would help him bond with her—and check out her digs.

Promptly at nine a.m. he turned into the long driveway at Heathfield and gave a low whistle. The woman had taste. She lived in a classic looking French country manor house surrounded by landscaped grounds and terraces. He glimpsed tennis courts and a blue green swimming pool behind the house. A rose garden, an English style manicured lawn, and a shaded creek winding through the property gave it the air of a true country estate.

I could live here, Mason thought.

Grace had tried three times that morning before she mustered the nerve to dial Mason's number. Even then she would've hung up if he hadn't answered the phone with such a soothing voice. He didn't sound like the hardened detectives on TV.

"I'm sure you'd rather not be seen at my office, so how about if I come to your place?" He paused for a moment and she heard paper rustling. "I can change my schedule around and be there by ten o'clock."

"Ten will be fine," she'd said.

It was almost a relief to have the decision out of her hands. Now she couldn't back out. After giving Mason directions to the estate, she quickly called Maria, the housekeeper, and gave her a day off with pay. She didn't want the woman gossiping about their personal business, nor did she know what to expect from Mason. In spite of his smooth voice, she pictured an African American version of Columbo—an older man in polyester pants and a seedy trench coat. Hopefully he wouldn't smoke cigars or spit on the floor.

She dressed casually in jeans and a blouse and then spent half an hour on her makeup and hair. Seeing Dajour's belongings in the bedroom made her feel guilty, so she went downstairs and busied herself in the kitchen. Why did *she* feel guilty when he was the one doing wrong? It didn't make sense.

When the doorbell rang Grace hurried to the front door and swung it open. "Hello, you must be –" She took a step backward and put one hand to her throat. On her doorstep stood the smoothest, finest black man she'd ever seen. Forget Columbo! This man wore khaki pants, a Brooks Brothers shirt, and a Rolex. He obviously worked out and took great care of himself. "Are you Mason?" she blurted.

"Yes, I'm Mason Harris." He rolled his eyes and smiled at her. "Let me guess. I'm not what you expected?"

"Not exactly. I thought you'd be...older." *And uglier,* she thought.

He extended his hand and Grace shook it. "Nice to meet you, Mason. Janet told me you're good at what you...do."

"She was right. I'm the best."

"Well haaaay." She stood aside so he could enter the house. Instead of waiting to be directed, he strolled inside and walked ahead of her, looking around.

"You have a beautiful home, Grace. Did you decorate it yourself?"

She hurried to get ahead of him so she could lead him through the garden room to the patio. "Thank you. And yes I did all the interior design. It's my specialty." She pointed to a glass topped table shaded by a striped umbrella. "I thought we'd sit out here and enjoy the lovely weather. Can I get you something to drink?"

"No, I'm fine, thanks." Mason helped her into a chair and then sat across from her and laid a slim leather case on the table. "Now, tell me Grace, what can I do for you?"

Grace had hoped for a few minutes of small talk to delay the inevitable, but Mason was obviously a man who like to get to the point. She took a deep breath. "Well, I need to find out if my boyfriend is cheating on me."

Mason folded his hands on the table. "What makes you think he is?"

"Just a feeling I have, plus some things here and there. He's working late all the time. We don't communicate the way we used to. And he wrote a check for 20 thousand dollars to a woman I've never heard of."

"Have you confronted him or asked him if he's cheating?"

"What's the use? He'd probably lie about it and I'd always have doubts."

Mason nodded. "I can see you're a smart lady. This way you'll know for sure, and if he's innocent he'll never realize you suspected him."

"Well, I hope you'll tell me it's all in my imagination," Grace said. "My last boyfriend cheated on me, so maybe I'm over reacting."

"Do you have pictures of your friend?"

"Of course. I'll just run inside and find one. Are you sure I can't fix you a drink?"

"No. Just the pictures." He settled back in the chair as she left.

Grace found the photo album in the bottom drawer of her

dresser and thumbed through it, looking for a recent picture of Dajour. Most of the photos showed them together during happier times. There was Dajour with his arm around her on the deck of a cruise ship, both of them sipping pina coladas. Another picture showed a backyard cookout at her parent's house with Dajour wearing an apron and grilling hamburgers. Finally, she found a photo of Dajour alone and took it from the book along with several others.

"Here you go." She handed the picture to Mason.

He stared at the photo, frowning. "Nice looking guy. How long have you two been together?"

"Three years, going on four." Grace joined him at the table and watched a pair of robins hop across the patio.

"He lives here, right?"

Grace nodded.

"You plan on marrying him?"

"I hoped so, but now I don't know." She stared across the lawn, avoiding eye contact with Mason. This was more painful than she'd expected.

Mason looked through the pictures, selected two, and passed the others back to her. "I won't be needing the rest of these."

"Do you need anything else?" Grace asked.

"Just his work address. I'll take care of everything else."

He handed her a pen and a pad of paper so she could write Dajour's business address. "It just feels so...strange. I've never done anything like this before."

He patted her hand. "You're doing the right thing, Grace. It's always better to be safe than sorry."

"These kind of cases—how do they usually turn out?"

He shook his head. "I'd like to say everyone lives happily ever after, but most of the time when a person thinks something's going on, they're right."

"And how much do you charge for your services?"

"Four thousand dollars a day."

"Oh yeah? That sounds awfully steep to me."

He shrugged. "That's my discount price. Like I said, I'm the best. I'll provide daily updates, photographs, and tape recordings. If you ever take this to court, you'll win."

"I see. Well, I suppose."

"Trust me, you won't regret it."

Grace reached inside her purse in slow motion. Besides the checkbook, she was trying to find some Kleenex, because something was in her eye. Mason handed her a white handkerchief.

"There's no need to cry," he said. "It'll be all right."

"I'm not crying. I think a bug flew into my eye." She sniffed and dabbed at her face with the handkerchief. "I never thought this would happen to me and Dajour." She scribbled a check for eight thousand dollars and handed it to Mason. "This should get you started. You'll call me soon? Use the cell phone number I gave you."

"I will," he said.

Grace walked him through the house and watched as he drove off in the red Mustang. Her thoughts were on Dajour. What would Mason find?

CHAPTER 11

A blonde walked into the sights of his binoculars, strutting along the sidewalk as though she owned it. Mason adjusted the knob and honed in on her chest. Not bad. As the woman moved out of range, he sipped cold Dunkin Donuts coffee from a paper cup and blinked sleepily. Perched on a rooftop across the street from Dajour's construction firm, he could watch the front entrance and also manage a view through the office windows. He'd been fighting off insects and pigeons for the past two hours—only one of the reasons he hated domestic cases.

Normally he'd let his apprentice deal with the tedium of surveillance, but this case was special. There was more at stake here than usual and he couldn't afford any slip ups. In fact, he'd stayed awake most of the night facing the dawning realization that he'd lost all enthusiasm for his profession. He was sick of skip-tracing and shutterbugging insurance frauds, and men who had sex with blonde trophy mistresses, and women who shagged the golf pro at the country club. His corporate clients were even worse. Everyone was stealing, but only the little guys got caught. The sharks at the top of the food chain paid his salary so they could devour the little fish at the bottom.

Grace could be his ticket to freedom. She was attractive, rich, and vulnerable—a perfect combination. Mason knew how to handle women like Grace, and he'd have her begging for it within a few weeks. That classy estate needed a man of his stature. He pictured himself lounging around the pool, Grace beside him in a bikini. There'd be dinner parties, pool parties, tennis games, and cruises on private yachts. Grace had the money and he had the social contacts. They'd be perfect together.

Mason sighed and checked his watch. None of this would come true if he didn't get busy and find Dajour. He looked at the photo again, shaking his head. Grace could do so much better—this guy was strictly blue collar.

On the street below, a Dodge Ram parked at the curb and the man in the picture climbed out, then opened the passenger side door for a young woman. Mason grabbed his camera and snapped three photos as the two of them entered the building. A few minutes later they appeared in Dajour's office, but the woman strolled over to the window and pulled the blinds. Mason got one good picture before she disappeared behind the shades.

"I've got you now, you dumb sucker!" He threw the equipment into a bag and ran for the rooftop door, which he'd propped open with a brick. He flew down three flights of stairs and made it to ground level just as Dajour and the woman left the building.

He had just enough time to jump in the Mustang and fire it up before Dajour turned the corner in his truck. Mason stayed two cars behind, expecting Dajour to head for an apartment building or hotel where he'd spend the rest of the day with his sweet young thing. The woman swiveled on the seat to face Dajour, laughing at something he'd said, then flipped down the mirror in front of her to check her makeup.

Dajour abruptly changed lanes and Mason had to slide the Mustang in front of a city bus to keep from losing his prey. The driver leaned on the horn and mouthed an obscenity. Mason gave him the finger. The white truck kept moving to the right and Mason guessed Dajour would be making a right hand turn within the next few blocks. A light changed ahead, leaving him idling in the traffic two cars behind the truck. He needed to get closer so he wouldn't be left behind when Dajour turned, but there was no way to pass the idiot ahead of him—a punk kid with a shaved head driving a panel van tricked out with throbbing speakers. The kid put his windows down, forcing everyone on the block to hear his music.

Mason pounded the steering wheel with his fist. He should've had Zack waiting in a second vehicle, but he hadn't expected Dajour to hit the streets so early. Most guys stayed in the office 'till noon before they took off with their women.

Knowing he'd have to sit through the light at least once, Mason did a quick check of his equipment. He wore a state of the art digital camera disguised as a wrist watch that would allow him to snap pictures and download them to his PC or Palm PDA. The camera contained a working watch as well. In his breast pocket he carried a tiny voice-activated tape recorder connected to a microphone that was cleverly disguised as an ordinary ink pen. Mason was good to go—if he could get close to Dajour and the woman.

When the light changed, Dajour zipped into the far right lane and made a quick turn. Mason was still in the wrong lane and had no choice but to keep driving, with the bus driver just itching to bump his rear end.

"Damn! He's gone!" Figuring it was lost cause, Mason hung a right at the next corner and worked his way back to the area where he'd last seen Dajour, a street lined with expensive specialty shops. To his amazement, the white truck sat in front of a jewelry store halfway down the block. Another miracle—a black BMW pulled out of a parking space right in front of him. Mason hopped out of his car and headed inside the store.

Dajour parked outside the store and waited while Roxanne dug through her purse for a comb. Why didn't women ever fix their hair ahead of time? It was one of those mysteries of life.

"So how much were you planning to spend on this ring?" Roxanne asked, peering at her reflection in the mirror.

He shrugged. "It doesn't really matter, as long as she likes it."

"How's everything been with you two?"

"She seemed to calm down a lot. She found out about the twenty thousand dollars I paid you and she didn't even trip." Dajour opened the door. "You ready to go? I need to finish this up and meet Smitty on one of construction sites. He's got a problem."

Dajour paused inside the store, feeling overwhelmed. The place reminded him of an old fashioned bordello—not that he'd ever seen one. Pink satin curtains framed the windows, held back by gold cords with tassels. About fifty grandfather clocks occupied the back of the store, and half of them were chiming ten o'clock. Glass cases filled with jewelry and watches lined the perimeter, each manned by a sales person.

The last time he'd set foot inside a jewelry store was to buy a battery for his watch. Fortunately, Roxanne knew her way around this alien world. He could tell she'd been there before. In fact, most of the clerks seemed to know her and one woman practically galloped to the front to wait on them.

"Roxanne! It's so good to see you. May I help you find something?" The woman had an overbite and spoke with a heavy Mainline accent. Old money from Philadelphia, he guessed. When she looked him over, her eyes reminded him of the shark in *Jaws*.

"We're here to look at rings," Roxanne said. "Just give us a few minutes."

"Of course." The woman backed away, but kept watching them.

"Does she think we're gonna steal something?" Dajour whispered.

Roxanne laughed. "No, she wants the commission."

Two other couples were looking at rings and an older woman tried on antique jewelry with her daughter looking on. As they settled in to examine rings, a single man entered the store and headed toward them. Dajour felt Roxanne stiffen.

"Damn, he's fine." She watched him saunter across the room.

Dajour nudged her. "Hey, pay attention here. Don't go wandering off on me." He pointed to a ring with a large diamond flanked by four sapphires. It was displayed on a tiny velvet cushion. "I like this one."

"Dajour, that's tacky. She's your future wife, not a gansta' rapper."

He pointed to a more conservative ring. "How about this one?"

Roxanne nodded, but her attention was on the strange man, who now stood across from them.

"Roxanne, you're not even looking."

"Huh?" She glanced at him. "Oh, I'm sorry baby. I wasn't paying attention. What about this one? It's a single carat, very expensive, but in good taste"

"I guess." Dajour thought the ring should have a couple more stones, but Roxanne was the expert. "You think she'd like it?"

"Hey, if you don't want to give it to her, give it to me. I'll take it."

Dajour shook his head. Before he could speak, the stranger slid toward them.

"No disrespect man, but your fiancée is gorgeous. How long have you two been together?"

Roxanne spoke up. "Oh, no no no! This is my friend. I'm helping him pick out a ring for his girlfriend."

Dajour decided to have a little fun. "You so crazy!" He put his arm around her. "She's a trip, man, always making jokes. We're actually engaged."

Roxanne elbowed him in the side. He smiled.

The guy smiled back. "Well, congratulations. I was hoping she was single." He checked his watch, a big ugly sucker with three or four dials on it.

"That's a bad looking watch," Roxanne said. "What does it do?"

He grinned at her, showing extremely white teeth. "Would you believe it's also a microwave oven?"

Dajour gave him a high five and the man left.

Roxanne turned on him right away. "You're sick, you know that? I could've had a date with that guy."

"He's not your type," Dajour said. "Too slick. You need somebody nice—like me."

"Yeah, but for just one night...." Roxanne stared at the door.

As they walked back to his truck, Dajour put one arm around Roxanne's shoulder. "Hey, thanks for helping me pick out her ring. I appreciate it."

"No problem, I threw that one in for free. Lord knows you men don't know shit when it comes to picking out rings."

He frowned and pulled the keys from his pocket. "Now hold up. I could've picked out the ring by myself if I wanted to. I just needed a second opinion."

"Yeah sure, you're right." Roxanne rolled her eyes.

Dajour dropped Roxanne at her car and drove straight to

the townhouse where Smitty and his crew were still working. With Billy off sick, he'd hired Low to fill in. The wife was still driving them crazy, changing her mind about one thing or another nearly every day. Smitty refused to deal with her, saying he'd be tempted to use a nail gun on her thick head, and Dajour spent at least an hour a day smoothing somebody's feathers.

He sighed with relief when he saw the woman's Chrysler wasn't parked in front of the house. Maybe he'd make it through one day without getting yelled at. He found Smitty hanging cabinets in the kitchen.

"Hey man, how's it going?" Dajour stepped over a can of nails.

Smitty set his tape measure down, perched on the edge of a sawhorse, and wiped his forehead with a rag. "Not too bad. Once we get these cabinets up I can lay tile around them put in the granite countertops. I'm gonna stay late tonight and get this done. Don't tell me that old heifer changed her mind again?"

"Nah. I haven't heard from her today. But I hear you've got a problem."

"C'mon outside." Smitty led him onto the back deck and closed the door. "It's Low. He's not working out. In fact he's the laziest so'm bitch I've ever met. This morning I caught him sleeping in the attic on an old rug."

Dajour sighed. "Man, I thought he'd work if we gave him a chance."

"That brother parties too much. I don't think he even went to bed last night. You can't do this kind of job with no sleep."

"Well, I ain't paying him to sleep on the job." Dajour

propped one foot on the railing. "You want to get rid of him?"

"We've got to," Smitty said. "My nephew's looking for work and he can start tomorrow."

"That's cool. You want me to talk to Low?"

Smitty shook his head. "I'm the foreman. I'll give him a day's pay and send him on his way. You just concentrate on keeping Mrs. Spencer off my butt."

"If only I could." Dajour took out his wallet and peeled off a bill. "Give this to Low and send him home."

"Yoohoo! Is anyone here?" A shrill voice echoed through the townhouse. "I brought some carpet samples."

"Speak of the devil." Smitty punched Dajour on the arm. "I swear that woman's got the hots for you."

Smitty found Low in the third floor bathroom, splashing cold water on his face from the sink.

"Hey, what's up? I finished sweeping."

Smitty had already checked the floors, and if Low had swept them he sure couldn't tell. The kid was allergic to work. He held out a fifty dollar bill. "Sorry, but we're not gonna need you any more. You can go on home.

Low took the bill. "That ain't right. Dajour hired me and you got no right to fire me. I'm gonna find him and—"

He tried to pass, but Smitty's big frame blocked the door. Smitty placed one meaty hand on the kid's chest. "Dajour knows about this. He ain't paying you to sleep all morning in the attic. You go on and get your stuff. You're done here. This is a man's job and you ain't up to it."

"Oh, so you gonna play me like that Smitty? You know I need this job."

"I know somebody else who needs it more, and he's willing to work." Smitty said.

Low slid past him. "Okay Smitty, but remember, aint no

telling what I might do. And don't think I'll forget." He called over his shoulder, "Old man, you ain't seen the last of me."

Smitty shook his head sadly. The dumb kid didn't even know what he'd lost.

Janet dangled one foot over the edge of the bathtub, holding a wine glass in one hand and the phone in the other. She'd hoped the call was from Mason, but Grace's voice came over the line.

"Girl, where'd you find that hunk?"

"He found me," Janet said. "His cousin lives next door and she set us up."

"Ya'll were really together?"

Janet sank lower in the hot water, letting it lap around her neck. "Well, not exactly. We spent one night together."

"So how was he?" Grace asked. "Come on, give it up!"

Janet paused. "Let's just say I could barely hobble in to work the next day, if you know what I mean."

"But he didn't call you afterwards?"

"Sure he did. He begged me to go out, but I blew him off. "

"Why not, girlfriend? I'd be camped on his doorstep."

"Because he's sneaky. He lied to me about his ex-girlfriend." This wasn't a topic Janet wanted to get into. It still rankled that Mason hadn't called her, but she had to let that go. Larger issues were are stake. "How you feeling about things?"

Grace sighed. "It's weird spying on Dajour. Now I feel funny around him, like I'm the one who messed up."

"Humph. I wouldn't. Hang on a sec—I've got another call." Janet set her wine glass on the edge of the tub and clicked the call waiting button on her phone. "Hello?"

"Janet? It's Mason. Have you spoken to Grace?"

She sat up straight, sloshing water onto the floor. "I'm talking to her now. What's happening?"

"Well, this morning I saw Dajour with another woman. I don't think he's cheating on Grace, but I have enough evidence to tell Grace he is. You know, the worse things look for Grace and Dajour, the better they look for us."

"You got that right," Janet said.

"I'm calling to see how you think she would take bad news if I gave it to her."

Janet leaned back again and stared at the ceiling. "If it has anything to do with Dajour, another woman, and bad news, she won't be taking it well. She's tied herself in knots over this thing as it is."

"That's what I figured. I'll just have to console her, won't I?" He laughed. "She can cry on my shoulder."

"Watch yourself, Mason."

"Now don't get all hissy, Janet. I remember who set me up with this gig." His voice was low and soothing.

"You'd better not forget. Grace listens to me and I can shut you down with just one phone call. We're in this together."

"To the end," Mason promised. "Tell her I'm almost ready to call, but don't say when. I want to collect another day's pay—and make her sweat. If I make this look too easy she won't appreciate me."

Janet clicked the phone back to Grace's call. "You still there?"

"I'm here."

"Speak of the devil," Janet said. "That was Mason and he wanted to get an idea about what state of mind you're in."

"Why would he need to know what state of mind I'm in?"

"I don't know, Grace. He called me on his cell phone and I couldn't hear very well. I'm sure he'll call you soon."

"I can't stand this waiting. I'm climbing the walls. Can you come out this afternoon?"

"Sorry," Janet said. "I've got an appointment to set up advertising for the business. Maybe tomorrow."

She hung up the phone, refreshed her wine glass, and added more hot water to the bath. Now Grace needed *her* instead of Dajour. The plot was unfolding exactly as she'd planned.

Not only that, she now had more dates than she could handle, thanks to Soul Mates. She personally interviewed the sexiest men and hooked them up with the best woman available—herself. Maybe that was a conflict of interest, but who was going to stop her?

CHAPTER 12

Dajour followed Grace into the kitchen after dinner and leaned against the counter, watching her scrape the plates. "Why don't you leave those dishes for Maria. Let's relax and watch TV like we used to." He held out his hand. "Come on. You look tired and stressed, and I know I am."

"So how was your day?" Grace asked. They were snuggled on the sofa, drinking beer and watching a ball game.

"I had to fire Low, that kid I told you about. He just didn't want to work."

"I'm sorry, baby. I know you hate firing people, but you can't let them take advantage of you."

"I never realized how hard it is to have your own business. Before, I only had to keep track of myself. Now I've got all these employees to worry about, plus their families, health insurance, payroll taxes. What a nightmare."

Grace took the remote from him and pressed the mute button. "You don't need to work, Dajour. In fact, neither of us has to work unless we want to. We could just travel and spend all our time together."

"No, baby. I can't let you support me." He patted her hand. "But maybe we'll go on a trip soon. In fact, there's something I've been meaning to ask you and this might be —"

The phone rang before he could spit out his marriage proposal to Grace. He had the ring in his pocket, but finding the perfect time and the right words proved harder than he'd expected. Now he almost welcomed the distraction.

Grace made a face and passed him the phone. "It's Smitty's wife. She says why isn't he home yet?"

He sighed. Smitty's wife kept him on a short leash and this wasn't the first time she'd called after work. It was a subtle way of saying she didn't want Smitty working overtime. He took the phone. "Doretha, Smitty wanted to finish hanging cabinets in the kitchen. He should be home any time. Give me a call in an hour if you haven't heard from him."

An hour later the phone rang again. This time Doretha sounded scared instead of angry. "It's almost bedtime and I don't know where Smitty's got to. That man always calls me when he's late. His dinner's all burned up."

"Okay, Doretha. I'll drive into town and check on him." Dajour tossed the phone onto the couch and heaved a sigh. "Now I'm Smitty's babysitter. Most likely he's in a bar somewhere, but she's gonna call every hour until I find him."

"I'll come with you," Grace said. "Maybe we can stop for ice cream after you send Smitty home."

It was a hazy summer evening with a slight breeze, a perfect night for a drive in the country. Miraculously, they avoided problems on the interstate and reached the city in record time. As he parked in front of the townhouse Dajour was surprised to see Smitty's truck outside the darkened building.

"Why would he be working without lights?" Grace asked. "This is spooky."

"Maybe his truck wouldn't start and he got a ride with somebody," Dajour said. "That must be it, but we'd better look around." He led Grace inside the front door and snapped on the lights.

She spun around, admiring the high ceilings and marble floors. "What a wonderful entryway. Have they hired a decorator?"

He snorted. "Don't even go there. The owner's wife would drive you crazy, just like she does me." Dajour led her through the living room to the kitchen, shouting as he walked. "Hey, man, your wife called. She says your dinner burned up on the stove."

Grace clutched his arm, throwing him off balance, and pointed into the kitchen. Smitty was sprawled on the floor between the sink and the butcher block, with a pool of blood congealed around his head. A bloody hammer lay on the countertop.

Dajour dropped to his knees. "Oh, man, I can't believe this! Grab a cell phone and call for help. Hurry!"

Smitty groaned, moving his head from side to side, but Dajour couldn't get him to talk or open his eyes. Smears of blood spattered the white cabinets and Smitty's red toolbox had spilled across the floor. He didn't move his arms or legs and Dajour prayed he wasn't paralyzed.

Dajour loosened Smitty's collar and unsnapped the leather tool belt from around his waist. "Smitty, stay with me, man. Don't give up. You're gonna make it, hang in there." He babbled on, hardly knowing what he was saying.

Grace came back in, waving the phone. "They're coming." She stepped closer and peered down at Smitty. "Is he alive?"

"He's still breathing. Thank God we got here in time."

The ambulance crew arrived within minutes. Two men in blue uniforms rushed into the townhouse lugging black bags filled with medical gear. After evaluating Smitty and asking Dajour few questions, they rolled the patient onto a stretcher and headed for the hospital. Dajour and Grace followed them down the front steps.

The presence of an ambulance and two police cars had attracted attention from neighbors who probably weren't used to seeing official cars outside their homes. A rookie cop hovered over an elderly woman wearing a silk bathrobe. She nodded and pointed toward the back yard as the policeman scribbled in a notebook.

Before Dajour could unlock his truck, a slim policewoman approached them. At least six feet tall, she wore three hoop earrings in her left earlobe. Her head was bare and smooth. She stripped off a pair of latex gloves, brushed the white talc off her ebony skin.

"I'm Sergeant Barney. I need to ask a few questions before you leave."

Dajour patiently answered questions about his status at the townhouse, the owner's name, and why Smitty was there. He kept one arm around Grace, who'd started to cry when she saw the paramedics load Smitty into the ambulance.

"The neighbors saw two men running out the back door just before dark and we found his wallet in the alley. Do you have any idea who might've done this?" Sergeant Barney looked at him through the lenses of her rimless glasses.

Dajour shook his head. "No. Everybody loves Smitty. He's about the nicest guy I know."

She cocked her head. "When I asked who hit him, Mr. Smith mumbled a few words. Sounded like he was trying to say 'hello.'"

"Low! He was saying *Low*. That's the guy we fired this afternoon."

At the hospital, Dajour and Grace waited in a lounge near the Emergency Room. On their way down the hall they'd glimpsed Smitty inside a curtained area. He lay on a narrow stretcher, his blood stained clothing piled on the floor. A woman was drawing blood from his arm, but Smitty didn't react to the needle. An orderly motioned for them to move on before Dajour got a better look.

He wanted to pace the floor, but Grace clung to his hand. "Do you think he'll make it?" she asked.

"Smitty's a tough old bird. He survived eighteen months in 'Nam, so he oughta be able to handle this. I'd like to get my hands on Low for just fifteen minutes." Dajour made a fist and visualized ramming it into Low's ugly face.

Doretha came through the swinging doors, followed by her youngest son, the seventeen year old who still lived at home. She headed straight for Dajour and flung herself into his arms. "I knew something was wrong. I just knew it. Is he gon' be all right?"

Grace patted her on the back. "I'll go find the doctor."

The ER doctor wore green scrubs and was so pale Dajour wondered if he lived in a cave. Even his eyelashes were blonde. After glancing at a clipboard, he crossed his arms and said, "Mr. Smith sustained a severe concussion, possibly a glancing blow from a hammer, but the CT scan doesn't show any serious brain damage. He also has three broken ribs, but no damage to the sternum and that should heal quickly. We'll monitor his neuro status, rehydrate him, and observe for cerebral edema. He can probably go home in a few days."

Doretha stared at him. "Can you say that in English?"

"He got a nasty bump on the head, Mrs. Smith, but he'll live. How's that?"

She nodded. "That's what I wanted to hear, Doc. Thank you."

Sergeant Barney was waiting in the wings to speak with them. She shook hands with Doretha and introduced herself. "We caught the guys who did this and I understand your husband put up a real fight. They attacked him with a hammer, but he got in a few good licks before he went down." She nodded to Dajour. "Low needed stitches and we had to bring him to the ER, which is why I'm here."

"I'm glad to hear it," Dajour said. "You mind if I have a few words with Low?"

"No way! We'll handle him. You know, a lot of things can happen to a punk like that in jail."

"You mean Bubba?" Dajour asked.

"Bubba and his cousins." Sergeant Barney smiled. She looked down at Grace, who was listening closely. "This your wife?"

"My girlfriend, Grace Johnson." Dajour put his arm around Grace.

"Why did Low do it?" Grace asked.

"Honey, two of the oldest motives known to man; revenge and money. He only got fifty bucks from your friend's wallet—barely enough to get high for a few hours." sergeant Barney looked Grace up and down, then smiled at Dajour again. "Well, I'd better get back to my prisoner."

Grace watched the policewoman leave. "That woman gives me the creeps—the way she looks at me."

Dajour laughed. "That's just her cop look. Maybe you've got a guilty conscience."

"Why would you say that?"

"Now don't get huffy with me, Grace. It was a joke."

He had a feeling Grace was about to go off on him, but luckily the pastor from Smitty's church arrived with a group of women from the congregation. Smitty and Doretha's grown children soon joined them, plus several grandkids. Everyone crowded around Doretha until Dajour wondered how the woman could breathe.

"I think we can go home now," he told Grace. "Doretha's in good hands."

"Just a minute." Grace picked up her purse, removed the checkbook, and started writing.

"What are you doing?"

"I'm writing her a check. She's gonna need money to get through this thing. It's the least we can do."

Dajour snatched the book from Grace's hands and shoved it back into her purse. "Are you crazy? Don't humiliate the woman by offering money in front of her friends. Besides that, she's my responsibility and I'll take care of her."

Grace's mouth trembled. "I didn't mean anything. It just seemed like a good idea to help her out a little bit."

Dajour took her arm and led her toward the door. "Baby, look over there." He pointed toward Doretha, who was dangling a grandchild on each knee. "That's all she needs right now—her family and friends. I know you meant well, but you've got to learn something: Money can't always fix things."

Dajour left for the hospital early the next morning. An hour later he called to tell her Smitty would be okay and the doctors said he could go home within a couple of days.

"That's great news," Grace told him. She knew Dajour worried about the people who worked for him, but she didn't much like Smitty and his wife. They were so—common.

"When will you be home?" she asked Dajour.

"Later in the day sometime. I'm meeting with the owners of the townhouse this morning. They're upset about what happened to Smitty."

Right after she hung up, Mason called and asked if he could drive out to the estate. She hadn't expected to hear back from him so soon. Grace nervously paced the floor in the living room, knowing whatever he told her would change her life.

When his Mustang pulled into the drive she was waiting at the front windows.

She opened the door before Mason could ring the bell. He held out a hand to shake hers, and his skin felt dry and hot. His hands looked like they'd never touched a piece of dirt or work in his life, unlike Dajour's hands. He was dressed in off white linen trousers and Gucci loafers, a cashmere vest over a white T-shirt.

"Good morning, Grace." He smiled at her. "How's life treating you?"

"I don't know yet." She led him into the family room, a cozy alcove with a brick fireplace where Dajour kept his favorite chair and the big screen TV he loved.

"Have a seat. Would you like an iced tea?" She paused in the doorway.

"I'm fine, actually." He settled on the taupe leather sofa and placed his attaché case on the floor. Mason seemed at ease, but her own nerves were taut as a piano wire.

"Have a seat, Grace." He patted the cushion beside him.

She perched on the edge of the sofa, facing him. "It's bad news isn't it?"

He nodded. "I'm afraid so. Grace, Dajour is cheating on you with another woman. I just need to verify the evidence I've gathered with you." He removed a tape player from his pocket and pushed a couple of buttons. "I recorded this yesterday morning in a jewelry store downtown."

Listening to Dajour's familiar voice, Grace put her head in her hands so Mason couldn't see her face. When the tape finished, he produced a series of digital pictures he'd taken. At the sight of Roxanne's face, she jumped to her feet.

"I know that bitch! I've seen her somewhere. That sonofabitch!" She paced the floor, raking both hands through her hair. Even though she'd prepared herself for the worst, Grace felt like her world had caved in. Her stomach heaved. She ran for the bathroom and hung over the sink, but the nausea soon passed—replaced by white hot rage. She splashed cold water on her fact, patted it dry with the guest towel, and returned to the family room.

Mason stood and led her back to the sofa. "Grace, calm down." He was beside her, rubbing her shoulders.

"Calm down? How could he do this to me?" She pulled at her hair. "After all this time together, all I've done for him, the shit we've gone through together! I can't believe it."

Mason put his arms around her. "Shhhhhhh."

"Don't shush me. I've got a right to be mad."

He stroked her hair. "Grace, maybe this is just a test. All couples have their ups and downs. You can get through this."

"Dajour should know by now not to test me. He swears up and down I'm crazy. If I were him, I wouldn't be trying to test a crazy person." Mason held her tighter, and Grace felt tears well up. She laid her head against his shoulder and sobbed. After a few minutes she pulled back and wiped her eyes. "I'm sorry. I'm sorry. I shouldn't be blowing up in front of you."

He pulled her back into his embrace and she hugged him back. His skin smelled tart and sweet, like a lemon mixed with honey. Having someone to lean on felt good.

"I'm gonna fuck him up," she said.

Mason released her. "Now Grace, you don't want to do anything drastic."

"The hell I don't." She ran out of the room, through the kitchen, and into the garage. Moments later she returned with a crowbar. "You just watch. As soon as he comes in here talking that shit, it's his ass, because I'm fucking him up today."

Mason laughed. "Where did you get that thing so fast?

You keep it in the hall closet or something?" He took the crowbar from her hands and laid it on the table. "You need to handle this a different way."

"You don't understand. I've been through way too much with Dajour to let him do me like this."

"I know. Men are funny. We take things for granted when we shouldn't. We abuse things we should be treasuring. And when everything blows up in our faces we look around and say, 'What the hell just happened?'" He pulled her down beside him on the couch. "You don't have to let him do you wrong, Grace. You just need to handle this with a little more tact."

She folded her arms and stared at him. "Sooooo? You're saying?"

"I'm saying, why get your hands dirty?"

"And that means?"

"Grace, by now people should be handling your business for you."

"What does that mean exactly?"

"All I'm saying is, your man obviously doesn't appreciate what he has."

"You've got that right."

"And Dajour shouldn't be treating you this way."

"I know all this, Mason. What's your point?"

He took one of her hands and held it. "I think your man needs to be taught a lesson."

"I know he does, so I don't understand why you just won't let me kick his ass. We both know he deserves it."

He touched the side of her face and spoke softly, almost in a whisper. "Let me take care of him for you. Free of charge."

She jumped to her feet and began pacing again. "I don't like the way you said that, Mason."

"What's wrong with the way I said it?"

"You sound like one of those Mafia hit men on TV. What are you—the Godfather?"

He laughed and kissed her on the nose. "You're a riot. I work with a couple of big guys who'll smack Dajour around and knock some sense into him for you. You shouldn't be in here all geared up to fight a man. Let another man handle that for you."

Grace stared out the window, picturing a couple of linebackers setting Dajour straight. "Fine. I'm willing to give it a try. But I don't want him hurt too bad—you know what I'm saying? Just put the fear in him."

"I'm glad you agree." Mason said.

"I don't want him in the hospital." Grace added. "Maybe a bloody nose or a black eye."

"You're a smart woman."

Mason was still holding her hand, which by now she felt perfectly comfortable with. He really seemed to care about her. Grace looked into his eyes and smiled. "I don't know about you, but I need a drink. You can relax, because Dajour won't be home for awhile and we have a lot to talk about."

Now that she'd made a decision about how to handle things with Dajour, Grace felt as though a weight had been lifted from her shoulders. Why not let Mason handle things? Dajour would learn his lesson and they'd go on as before.

She crossed the room to the wet bar and held up two crystal glasses. "You want anything?"

"What do you have?" Mason was back on the sofa...

"The good stuff."

"Like?"

"Well, what's your taste—vodka, whiskey?

"Scotch." She tilted her head to one side and studied the bottles. "I got some Johnny Walker Blue that's older than your grandmother."

Mason threw back his head and laughed. "Sounds great."

She poured the golden liquid into two glasses, set them on a tray, and placed it on the table in front of the sofa.

He picked up his glass, sniffed it, and took a sip, rolling it around on his tongue. "That's good stuff, Grace. I admire your taste."

"So how much is this going to cost me?" she asked.

Mason shook his head. "You've already paid me enough. I'll take care of this as a friend."

"Who are these men?"

"It's best that you don't know." Mason had the most incredible smile. Sexy, when you got right down to it. "Do you want to be around when he gets taken care of?"

Grace sipped her drink, considering. "Yeah, I do. I wanna see the look on his face when they mention that woman's name."

Mason laughed. "When do want it to happen?"

"This weekend—the sooner the better, before I have time to change my mind."

"And where?" Mason asked.

"How about one of the clubs? That'll make it look better."

"I like the way you think. Which club will it be?

"How about Y2K 9, in the city?"

"Yeah, that's perfect. Let him go out in style." Mason's eyes looked ice cold for a moment, then he smiled at her. "How many guys do you want?"

"Well, Dajour can whup some ass when he wants to, so maybe you'd better have three."

"Three it is." Mason held up his glass and Grace clinked hers against it. "To love and revenge," he said.

CHAPTER 13

Dajour spent a couple of hours at the townhouse, smoothing the wife's ruffled feathers and cleaning the kitchen. The woman made a show of being concerned about Smitty, but she mostly worried about blood on her kitchen cabinets, a nick in the floor tile caused by Smitty's tool box, and the embarrassment of having police cars at their new home before they even moved in.

"The neighbors will think we're trailer trash," she muttered, staring at the adjacent house from the front window. She spun around and smiled brightly. "I'm sure you won't let this unfortunate incident put you behind schedule, Mr. Wright. And I trust you'll replace those damaged floor tiles at no cost to us."

"I'll take care of everything," he promised, feeling like a character out of Uncle Tom's Cabin. The woman was racist *and* an overeducated snob without the slightest bit of common sense. In a way he felt sorry for her.

Luckily, Smitty's nephew showed up and brought a friend with him. Both men seemed to know their way around and Dajour got them started right away. By the time everything was sorted out, Dajour decided to go home for the rest of the day. He'd slept poorly the night before and he wanted to see Grace.

Dajour hated Route 95 with a passion. Sometimes he wished they still lived in an apartment so he didn't have to fight traffic twice a day. He'd been perfectly happy in the brownstone. Now Grace bitched and complained because they never spent time together, but their new house was so far out he practically had to live in his truck. He checked the rearview mirror and moved into the right hand lane, which was moving faster than the other two lanes. Immediately, traffic slowed to thirty miles per hour.

He pulled the engagement ring from his pocket and held it in the palm of his hand, letting sunlight sparkle on the diamonds. Today he'd definitely pop the question to Grace, assuming he could catch her in a good mood. After seeing Smitty and Doretha together at the hospital he'd decided not to wait. Life was too short and a person never knew what might happen.

Grace refilled her glass, set the bottle on the coffee table, and took another sip of fine Scotch. Her face felt flushed she was getting a bit tipsy, but who cared? She deserved a few drinks after what Mason had just told her.

"Dajour is one stupid brother," Mason was saying. If I had a woman like you, I wouldn't be fucking around on her like that."

"Yes you would. If I was with you, I'd just put your picture by the bed and when my friends came in I'd point to it and be like, 'That's my man right there.'"

Mason smiled and looked down. "Janet told you."

"Yeah." She grinned at him.

"What else did she tell you?"

"She told me you're sneaky."

Mason shrugged. "I'm a detective. I'm supposed to be sneaky."

"Is that why you two didn't see each other again?"

"No." He stared into his glass, swirling the golden liquid.

"What was it, if you don't mind me asking?"

"I don't know. We just didn't click right. Janet seems like she wants to control everything. She's always got a plan. I like a woman who's more laid back."

"Oh, I see. If you were my man, I think I'd be pretty laid back, if you know what I mean," Grace said, and immediately wanted to bite her tongue. Was she flirting? Or was she making a fool of herself?

Mason set his glass down and scooted closer. "I really admire you. You're so strong about all this."

"That's because you're here. After you leave, I'll probably cry myself to sleep with Dajour lying right there beside me."

"Look, if you need me, I'm here."

Grace nodded, feeling her eyes start to water again. "I know."

Mason brushed away her tears with his fingertips, then leaned forward and softly kissed her cheek. She turned her face and their lips met. His mouth felt good—soft and dry and firm. He tasted so good. She leaned against him and felt his body press against hers.

"Can we go upstairs?" he whispered.

Before she could answer, the kitchen door opened and closed. Grace pulled away from Mason. "Shit! Dajour's back home! You've got to go!"

Mason grabbed his attaché case and sprinted for the front door. Grace heard the Mustang roar down the driveway just as Dajour stepped into the room.

Janet waited in her car outside Mason's office for almost an hour before he returned. He parked the T bird two slots in front of her Mazda without even noticing her. *Some detective*, she thought. This time she didn't hide under an awning; she followed Mason to the door and stopped him before he could enter the building.

"Hi!" she said, tilting her sunglasses down so he could see her eyes.

"Janet! What brings you here?" Mason didn't look happy to see her, but it didn't matter at all. This was business and she didn't trust him an inch.

"I was in the neighborhood and thought I'd check in with you," she lied. "How did things go with Grace this morning?"

He pointed to a city park across the street. "Let's walk over there where we can talk in private."

"So tell me everything," Janet said as she and Mason walked under sun-dappled trees in the park. The afternoon was hazy, marked by a humid breeze that smelled of rain. A man wearing bright red suspenders sat on a bench tossing peanuts to a flock of blue and gray pigeons.

They circled the birds to keep from scaring them and Mason steered her around a pile of dog poop on the sidewalk. "You were right," he said. "She didn't take the news well. In fact, she brought a crowbar from the garage and said she was gonna use it on Dajour."

"No way!" Janet stared at him. "I hope you talked her out of it. We don't need that kind of trouble."

"Naturally, I calmed her down. By the time I left she agreed to let me handle everything. It'll go down tomorrow night at the club, just the way we planned." He moved aside to let a boy on a skate board rumble past them. "You don't seem to have much faith in me."

They came to a fountain and Janet sat on the edge, staring into the water. Hundreds of glittering coins lay on the bottom of the pool, tossed there by people who wanted to change their lives. How stupid, she thought. Wishing didn't make things happen. You had to take action if you wanted the world to change.

She had a sudden thought. "You didn't come on to her, did you?"

"Of course not." Mason's answer was a little too fast.

"You did, didn't you? You bastard!" She splashed water at him, speckling his linen trousers.

"Whoa, Janet! Back off. I kissed her one time, that's all. I want Grace to trust me, depend on me. I saw an opportunity and I took it."

"You're a piece of work, Mason."

He shrugged. "She's a fine looking woman, but so are you. When we get this business thing out of the way who knows what might happen?"

Janet knew the man was playing her, but she couldn't help smiling. "We'll see about that, Mason. You just keep your pants zipped for now."

Dajour stood in the doorway, looking around. He could swear he smelled men's cologne and Grace looked rumpled. In fact, she looked half drunk. "You here by yourself?" he asked. "Who's Mustang was that out front?"

She attempted to stand, balanced herself against the arm of the couch. "Fuck you man. Asking me all these questions."

He strode into the room "What you been doing in here?"

"I've been getting fucked up, what does it look like I've been doing, you bastard?"

He raised both hands as though warding off a blow. "I give up! Now can you tell me what this is all about?"

"Don't play stupid with me, you son of a bitch." Grace swayed, caught herself, and sat down hard on the cushions.

Dajour held out one hand as though to steady her, than thought better of it and stayed where he was. "Grace, you're drunk. You stink and you're drunk. I'm not listening to anything you have to say until you're sober."

She staggered toward him, raised her arms, and pounded on his chest. "You don't listen to anything I have to say anyway. Why should I even try!"

Dajour saw she was mad and crying at the same time. He grabbed her arms and peered into her face. "You were fine when I left this morning. What the hell's going on with you. Are you upset about Smitty? He's gon' be fine."

"I don't give a rat's ass about Smitty."

He looked past her and saw two glasses on the table. "Who you been drinking with?"

Her eyes widened. "Janet. And that was her new car you saw. Who else would I be drinking with? You're never here anyway, so why does it even matter to you?"

"Janet?"

"Yeah, Janet. Now get off of me." She jerked her arms loose.

"You know, if I didn't spend two hours a day sitting in traffic I'd be here more. Is this all about me not being here all the time or is it something else?"

"Oh, is there something you want to tell me?"

"I'm asking you Grace."

"Fuck you! I'm going to bed." She staggered out of the room, still sniffling, and moments later he heard her go upstairs.

Dajour slipped the diamond ring back into his pocket and turned on the television.

Grace awakened at three a.m. Saturday morning with the worst hangover of her life. Dajour hadn't come to bed, but she didn't have the strength to look for him. She crawled into the bathroom and lay on the tile floor beside the toilet. At four a.m. she pulled a bath towel off the rack and covered herself with it. At five she grabbed another towel for a pillow. After that she slept for a few hours, but awakened with a massive headache. Her temples throbbed with each heartbeat and the inside of her mouth tasted like the floor of a chicken coop. She promised herself she'd dump the rest of that Scotch down the drain before the day was over.

She turned on the water, brushed her teeth, and then took an long, steamy shower, letting the hot water pound her body until her skin stung. At first her mind wouldn't function, but vague memories soon returned: Mason touching her face; the tape recording of Dajour; drinking too much of that damn Scotch. And finally, pounding on Dajour's chest and the bewildered, hurt expression on his face.

She'd been a real bitch, and although she couldn't remember her exact words, Grace knew it wasn't good. She also remembered kissing Mason and the narrow escape when Dajour walked in. Was that how it had been between Dajour and his woman? A few drinks together and bingo—the hormones kicked in? Maybe she needed to show him a thing or two about hormones.

A fresh breeze ruffled the bedroom curtains. It would be a gorgeous day, sunny and warm with just a hint of autumn in the air. The world was so beautiful—why was her life such a mess?

After swallowing a couple of Tylenol, Grace did her hair, put on makeup, and walked downstairs wearing one of Dajour's T-shirts. She found him sleeping on the couch with the TV on, the remote balanced on his stomach. She covered him with an Afghan and headed for the kitchen. Cooking always soothed her nerves.

Coffee—strong and black—was the first priority. Then she mixed batter for pancakes, fried half a package of turkey bacon, and prepared the batter for omelets. Dajour loved her cheesy omelets, and this morning she needed all the help she could get.

Dajour awakened to the scent of coffee mingled with bacon. Sounds from the kitchen told him Grace was cooking breakfast, but he didn't feel like facing her just yet. Instead, he headed for the upstairs bathroom, where the glass shower door and mirrors were still steamy from her shower.

The night before he'd checked on her a couple of times, but she hadn't moved when he came into the bedroom and turned on the lights. He had no idea what had set her off, but she was a mean drunk. He'd microwaved a frozen dinner and spent Friday night watching TV and feeling sorry for himself. Around nine, he called Miss Charletta.

"Dajour, is that you? Just a minute." She turned down the TV and came back on the line. "I'm glad you called. My knees are so bad I can hardly get around. I want you to drive me to the doctor's office Monday morning."

"Sure, Mama. I'll stop by around nine. How you doin' otherwise?"

"What you calling this late at night for? Shouldn't you be in bed with that woman?"

"Grace, Mama. Her name's Grace and she went to sleep early."

Dajour, you know what? You need to either marry that woman or move out. What you're doing ain't right."

He groaned. "Mama, I didn't call you to get lectured."

"You and Miss Thang have a fight?"

"Something like that."

"Well, here's my best advice. You need to either get married or move on. She's not gonna feel secure until you give her a ring and a date."

"How do I know she's the right one?"

Mama huffed into the phone. "Baby, we don't know nothing for sure in this life. You been with Grace a long time, so there must be something to it. And while you're at it I need me some grandbabies."

"Yes, Mama." Dajour grinned.

"But not before you're married. You got that?"

"I hear you, Mama."

After they hung up, Dajour wandered back upstairs, took the ring from his pocket, and held it to the light. Roxanne had made a good choice, he decided. The diamonds were tasteful, but not flashy. Hearing Grace turn over on the bed, he put the ring inside a blue velvet box and left it inside his sock drawer. Someday soon, when Grace wasn't on his back, he'd propose.

He took a shower, snagged the newspaper from the living room, and wandered into the kitchen. Grace stood in front of the stove wearing nothing but one of his oversized T-shirts. Damn, but she did look nice. He grabbed a carton of orange juice from the refrigerator and opened the cabinet to take out a glass.

"Good morning baby," Grace said.

Dajour ignored her. He dropped two slices of bread into the toaster.

"I apologize about yesterday." She held a spatula in one hand. Her eyes were swollen like she'd been crying. "You don't have to make toast. I'm cooking already."

He sat at the table and opened the newspaper with a flourish, still ignoring her. Grace continued frying bacon, placing the browned slices on a paper towel to drain. It smelled good and he was starved. She set two plates loaded with food on the table.

"If you don't eat this it'll just go to waste."

With a sigh Dajour folded the paper and picked up his fork. Grace smiled at him.

"Grace, how long have we been together now? About three, three and a half years, right?"

She lowered her eyes. "As far as I know."

"And we still have problems. Sometimes I'm afraid for us." He paused to crumble bacon onto his omelet. "But somehow I think...I *know* everything's going to work out between us."

Grace started to cry, hiding her face with her hands. "I don't know what's happened to us, Dajour. I felt so much closer to you when we didn't have anything. Now it seems like you're slipping further and further away from me."

"And there you go, imagining things." He reached across the table for her hands. "I'm not going anywhere. You're my woman, you'll always be my woman." He touched the back of her hand to his lips. "Why don't we go out or something? Let's focus on me and you for once."

Grace stood and walked toward him, still crying. Dajour shoved his plate aside and pulled her onto his lap. She clung to his shoulder as he picked her up and carried her upstairs. Breakfast could wait.

CHAPTER 14

This wasn't the first time Dajour had carried Grace upstairs, but today he noticed something different. This time her eyes never left his; she didn't look down or stare at the ceiling. Before, he'd always had the feeling that she worried a bit about her own safety.

This time it seemed as if she didn't care.

He placed her on the bed, turned his back, and began removing his own clothing. He paused to watch in the dresser mirror as she slipped the T-shirt over her head and tossed it onto the floor. Then she lay on her back atop the gold satin bedspread, watching him strip. He made a show of removing his boxer shorts, twirling them around on one finger, and tossing them into the corner. Grace didn't say a word, but her eyes glistened.

There was something different about his woman this morning, but he couldn't quite put his finger on it—though he intended to try.

As he walked toward her, Grace let him know she had no interest in foreplay. She grabbed his wrist and pulled him on top of her. He didn't even have time to fondle her breasts before she guided him inside her. Then she began rotating her hips while at the same time pushing them forward and backward.

Dajour found himself completely enthralled by her movements, amazed at the surge of animal instinct he felt. He wanted to use her for his own immediate physical release.

He plunged into her over and over, crying out with pleasure. Then, suddenly stopping all movement, Grace brought him back from the edge and commanded him to slowly pull out. Gasping for air, he did as she asked.

As soon as they were separated, Grace rolled Dajour over on his back, placed one hand around him, and started touching herself with her other hand. While stroking him she quickly achieved an orgasm that wracked her body with waves of delight. He cuddled her in his arms for a few moments as their mouths locked together in a long, passionate kiss.

Suddenly, she mounted him from above and began a wonderful pumping action. Dajour reveled in the silky wetness of her body, the pleasure of her womanhood. He held onto her breasts as she bent over to kiss him again.

The animal instinct was gone, replaced by a surge of intense love for this woman who pleased him so much. A fog of sensual delight lifted his soul and he welcomed it, reached for it. Then, somewhere far away, he heard Grace say, "Now!" He climaxed with the power of an erupting volcano.

It left him so weak he could barely move his limbs. He lay there, holding Grace in his arms, waiting for his strength to return.

"I love you," she whispered. "Did I do alright?"

"Hmmmm," he kissed her again. "It just keeps getting better. I love you too, Booby."

An hour later, Dajour propped himself onto one elbow and traced the curve of Grace's cheek with his finger. They lay tangled in the satin sheets on their bed, relaxed and exhausted from the intense lovemaking. During his nap, Dajour had decided Grace's outburst from the day before was his fault. A woman like Grace needed to know she was loved and needed, but he'd let himself get preoccupied with other things. He looked into her lovely brown eyes. "I know I haven't been putting the kind of time I should into our relationship."

She shook her head. "No, it's my fault. I should be more understanding. I'm just being selfish, that's all."

He leaned forward and kissed her full lips. "I'm sorry."

"Me too. And I won't be drinking any more Scotch. I poured it down the drain."

Dajour laughed. "You'd better stick to beer from now on." He looked into her eyes for a moment. "I should work this morning, but I'm taking the day off. We need some time together. Besides, it's the weekend. Who works on weekends besides me, anyway?"

Grace smiled at him and stretched both arms above her head. "I promise I'll keep you occupied."

"Today it's all about us, and tonight it's all about us."

"Let's leave everything here—cell phones, pagers. People will just have to do without us for one day."

Dajour walked to the dresser, scooped up their cell phones and his two way pager, and dumped everything inside the top drawer. "That's where they'll stay until Monday."

The bedside phone rang. They looked at each other and laughed. Grace patted the bed. "Let the machine get it. You come on back here, because I've got something for you."

Later, Dajour made a quick call from the kitchen phone to Roxanne. "Have you got everything ready?"

"I just picked up your tickets and the whole packet's ready to go. You can use those tickets anytime within the next year. So, have you proposed yet?"

"I meant to last night, but Grace is acting all crazy again. I'm gonna wait 'till after the weekend, see how we get along."

"That's procrastination, Dajour. You know you want to marry her. Just do it!"

"Monday. I'll ask her on Monday I promise. We're going to a club tonight. How about I meet you there and you can leave the stuff in our car?"

"Eleven o'clock," Roxanne promised. "Then you'll have everything you need, and I'd better not hear any more excuses."

Janet glared at her cell phone and tossed it onto the front seat of her car. She'd called Grace half a dozen time since the night before and left messages, but the bitch hadn't bothered calling back. She swerved her car, narrowly missing a kid on a bicycle.

Grace should've called her right after Mason left. The fact that she hadn't called made Janet nervous. What if Grace and Dajour made up? That would ruin everything. She pressed speed dial and called Mason's number.

"Mason? It's Janet. I can't get in touch with Grace. I'm trying to verify where she's going to be tonight and I can't catch up."

"Don't sweat it. I'll always know. It's my job to keep track of this guy. If I want him, I'll go and get him."

Janet sighed. Enough of this detective mumbo jumbo. "Shouldn't we make sure Grace didn't change her mind? She's half crazy, you know."

"They'll be at the club like I said. Their house is bugged, so what are you worried about?"

She stopped for a red light, hit the brakes too hard, and lurched forward. "You wired their house?"

"Something like that. So chill out and enjoy the day."

"And I'll see you at the club tonight?" The light turned green and Janet accelerated with the traffic.

"It would be best if you stayed away, Janet. We don't want Dajour getting suspicious."

"No way! I'll just say hello to Grace and keep my distance."

Mason sighed. "Don't screw this up. I'll be around, but you won't see me."

Mason sat behind his desk on Saturday morning—unusual for him, but this was a job he wouldn't handle from home. With their bald heads, steroid biceps, and loud clothes, the three Ukrainians in front of him resembled triplets separated at birth. All three muscle bound necks sported thick gold chains. Gorillas for hire. Hit men. He'd worked with these guys before on collection jobs and putting the squeeze on people, but this was the first serious job they'd done for him.

"Hey, Mason!" Borysko, the leader, cracked his knuckles. "So what's this mark look like? We don't wanna get the wrong guy." His predatory grin revealed a perfect set of false teeth.

Mason handed him a picture. "This is your target. Take a good look now and leave the photo with me."

Borysko passed the photo to Ivan and Burian. "Half now and half later, right?"

Mason opened the desk drawer, removed a stack of bills, and slid them across the desk. Borysko slipped the money inside his jacket without counting it. He nodded. "We're good to go."

After they left, Mason walked to the window and watched the three cousins climb into a sinister looking black Cadillac with tinted windows. He was playing with the big boys now.

Grace and Dajour made a list of things to do, including several errands they'd put off and a stop at Smitty's house. When they parked in front of Smitty's Grace wanted to wait outside, but Dajour insisted she come with him. "There's something here I want you to see."

Smitty and Doretha lived in a white frame house that was

almost identical to the house Grace's parents owned. The yard featured pink flamingos, a white goose wearing a cape, and a wooden duck with spinning wings. Plastic grass carpeted the front steps.

The interior of the house was one of the ugliest Grace had ever seen. The living room was covered in shag carpeting so deep she could hardly see her shoes. The couches and armchairs were brown with orange flowers, but the coffee table, end tables, and enormous home entertainment armoire were a shiny metallic black. A wet bar, encased in mirrored glass and lit by 150-watt bulbs was built into the corner and painted black to match the armoire. Dozens of family pictures lined the walls and occupied every inch of table space.

Smitty lay under a quilt on the couch, his head wrapped in a thick bandage with dark red blood stains on the front. He held out his hand to Dajour, but winced with the movement.

"Don't get up," Dajour said. "I can see it hurts."

Grace shuddered and took a seat in one of the armchairs, moving several hand crocheted pillows so she could fit. Dajour perched on the arm of her chair.

"So, they let you come home early," Grace said, trying to make conversation.

Doretha bustled into the room carrying four tall glasses filled with lemonaide. She wore a bright blue smock with embroidery on the front and open toed house slippers. "The doctor said Smitty's got the hardest head he ever saw." She flopped on the end of the couch and Smitty put his legs across her lap. She massaged his feet through the covers.

"How you plan on finishing that job without me?" Smitty asked. "I hate that I didn't get those cabinets hung."

"I'll manage. Don't even think about coming to work for awhile. Your nephew can fill in and I'll hire on a couple more guys next week."

"Smitty can stay home 'till he starts getting on my nerves," Doretha said.

Smitty tried to grin, but it turned into a grimace. He rubbed his head. "I hear Low's already back on the street. One of his girlfriends paid the bail."

"Hard to believe what folks'll do for money," Doretha said. "The boy needs a good ass-whipping."

"That he does." Dajour drained his glass and set it on the lacquered tray. "We'll get out of your way now. I just wanted to let ya'll know you can call us if you need anything."

"I'm gon' fatten this man up while he's home," Doretha said. "You won't hardly know him when he comes back to work."

As they walked back to the car carrying a plate of cookies from Doretha , Dajour put his arm around Grace and whispered, "I know this house isn't much, but it sure is full of love. That's what I wanted you to see."

"Why?" she turned to look at him.

"Because it's what I want for us."

They stopped at Kentucky Fried Chicken and picked up enough food to last all afternoon, then drove to Rock Creek Park, a 1700 acre National Park in historic Georgetown. Dajour located a picnic spot in a shaded glen and spread a quilt on the grass below the trees while Grace unpacked their wicker basket. Along with bottles of water they enjoyed fried chicken, potato salad, rolls, and cupcakes. Afterwards, they waded in the creek, splashing and playing in the rapids and skipping rocks across the clear pools.

Dajour collapsed on the quilt and Grace settled beside him with her head propped on his stomach. "This is nice," she said. "Why don't we do this more often?" She wiggled her bare toes at a butterfly.

"We will," he said. "From now on I'm taking weekends off."

"Maybe we'll buy a boat. Would you like to sail with me?" Grace rolled onto her stomach, picturing white sails, boating clothes, and picnics at sea.

"Sounds like work to me. How about a Donzi 28 ZX?"

"You mean a Don Johnson boat? And how much would that cost?"

"Probably more than my new truck." He caught a maple leaf drifting down from the treetops. "I'm just kidding. I'd be happy in a rowboat with you."

"Kayaks! We'll get kayaks and learn to whitewater," Grace said. "And how about that bike rental place we passed? Let's be real tourists and see everything."

They rented two bicycles for an hour and followed a signed bicycle route through the park. Next, they toured The Old Stone House on M Street, built in 1765. Grace especially enjoyed the gardens where she picked up ideas for the estate.

Dajour was ready to head home, but Grace discovered the walking tour of Black Georgetown, a fifteen block area called Herring Hill where over one thousand black families lived from the mid-to-late 1800s. Most of them worked as gardeners, cooks, and stable help for the white population. During President Franklin D. Roosevelt s administration, black homeowners were offered high prices by real estate dealers who turned over the renovated houses to white residents.

Dajour was especially taken by the Mount Zion United Methodist Church, the oldest black congregation in the District of Columbia and a stop on the Underground Railroad. He circled the building, touching the aged bricks and admiring the architecture. "They really knew how to build in those days," he told Grace. "Black workers and church members constructed this entire building."

"Maybe we'll go to church here some day," Grace said. "That would make both our mamas happy."

"I'd enjoy that, Booby." He wrapped his arms around her. "I'd like going to church with you. But right now I'd like a hot shower and a nap."

They burst in the door that evening, tired and laughing. Dajour flung himself onto the couch and propped his feet up. "Still wanna go out tonight?"

"Why not? I've got a new dress in the closet. Let's do it up."

"Cool. Come snuggle with me and we'll take a little nap."

She settled in his arms on the wide couch. "We still up for Adam's Morgan?"

"How about the Gardens?" Grace asked. "They've got a new band this week."

"The Gardens it is," Dajour said. "Let's have TexMex for dinner and then we'll dance it off."

When Dajour pulled up in front of the nightclub he noticed three tough looking white guys talking to the bouncer outside, slipping a wad of bills into his hand. The men lingered a moment before stepping inside the club. Strange, he thought. The bouncer just go paid off for something.

He tossed the Bentley's keys to the valet and took Grace's arm. She looked ravishing in diamond earrings, a matching necklace, and a black velvet dress that hugged her curves. "We're going to have a good time tonight," he said.

The dance club was packed full of people swaying to Muddy Waters' Jealous Hearted Man. Downstairs in the bar, people sat at tables where they could talk and flirt over drinks. Grace took Dajour's hand and dragged him onto the dance floor. They danced until the band took a break and then drifted over to the bar. Dajour grabbed a stool for each of them and Grace sat beside him, mopping the sweat off her forehead with a napkin. He leaned over and kissed her on the lips.

"You're beautiful tonight."

Someone tapped Grace on the shoulder and she turned to see Janet standing behind them, holding her usual glass of wine.

"Janet! How you doing?" Grace swiveled in her seat while Dajour carried on a conversation with the bartender.

"I'm great. The question is—how are you? I've been trying to call you all day."

"We went out to do some stuff and decided to leave the phones and pagers behind." Grace stirred her drink. "We're kind of starting over."

Janet leaned forward and glanced at Dajour. "But what about—?"

Before Janet could finish, Dajour grabbed Grace's arm and pulled her off the stool. "Baby there's somebody I want you to meet. Come on."

Grace waved a quick goodbye to Janet and trotted beside him. "That was rude, Dajour. Janet and I were talking. And besides that, you didn't even speak to her."

"Janet's not my favorite person and she's no friend to you, Grace. Trust me on that." Dajour looked into her eyes. "Do you believe me?"

Grace glanced back at Janet, who'd sidled up to a single guy at the bar. "I guess so, but is there something I don't know about?"

"I'll tell you later. How about another dance?"

"Right after I get back from the ladies room." Grace headed to the restroom downstairs, which was usually less jammed than the one near the dance floor. She spent a few minutes combing her hair and freshening up, then headed back to Dajour. Halfway across the room she stopped in her tracks. Looking oh so fine, Mason stood near the back exit with his arm draped around an attractive woman who was laughing at something he'd said.

Grace's eyes widened in terror. The fuzzy memories from their meeting the day before clicked into place. What had she done?

She waved at Mason and rushed toward him, but a throng of people moving toward the stairs cut her off. By the time she waded through the crowd, Mason and the woman had disappeared. She rushed back to the pay phone outside the bathroom and rummaged through her purse for change. She dropped the purse, scattering lipstick, a comb, her reading glasses, and everything else onto the floor. A couple of women leaving the bathroom stared at her as she wildly grabbed change off the floor until she found thirty five cents.

The pay phone was occupied by a man arguing with his wife, giving the poor woman half a dozen reasons why he'd be home late. Grace hovered nearby and checked her watch, making it obvious she needed to make a call. Finally he slammed down the receiver and brushed past her. "Lady, I hope you have better luck than I did."

Grace dialed Mason's cell phone, praying he'd answer. He didn't. She called his home and his office, but naturally he wasn't there. Finally she ran back upstairs searching for Dajour.

He wasn't where she'd left him. She waited while the bartender served a couple at the other end of the bar. He caught her eye and approached, wiping his hands on a white linen towel. "Someone came and told Dajour there's a problem with your car. He said to wait here and he'll be back in a few."

Dajour followed the valet to the parking garage and down the ramp to the lowest level. "I never had problems with the car before. What's wrong with it?"

"I don't know, Sir. They just sent me to find you. Here's your car."

"Well, I don't see anything wrong with it. What's going on?"

The kid in the red jacket shrugged, then backed away and seemed to vanish. The three men he'd seen paying off the bouncer stepped out of the shadows. The guy in front looked like the Incredible Hulk. Besides wearing too many gold chains, he had a diamond embedded in one of his front teeth.

Dajour breathed a silent prayer of thanks that Grace wasn't with him. "Hey man, what's up?" he asked the front man. "I'm not looking for trouble. You can have my stuff." He fished a wallet and car keys from his pocket and placed them on the car. "Enjoy my ride. The gas tank's full."

"This is not about your car. We may take your money— afterwards."

The man rolled his R's with a distinct foreign accent. Probably Russian. Dajour had no idea why the Russian mafia would want him. "I think you're making a mistake," he said, sidling toward a nearby panel van. He might stand a fighting chance if he had something at his back.

"You're name is Dajour?"

Dajour nodded. "Yeah, but I don't even know any Russians."

"Then no mistake."

Dajour balanced on his toes as the men stepped forward. He didn't like fighting, but he'd won a few bar brawls in his day. If that's what it came to, he'd take them on. "Hey, at least make this a fair fight. Let me take you one at a time."

"We no get paid to fight fair."

"Whatever somebody paid you, I'll double it."

"Sorry. It don't work that way."

The men surrounded him before he could reach the van. He glanced wildly around the garage. No one else was in sight, nothing handy he could use for a weapon. Resigned to getting beat up, Dajour pretended to sink to his knees. When the big guy moved in, he slugged him in the face, hearing the man's nose crunch under his fist. Swinging a hammer for ten years had helped him develop quite a punch.

Stunned, the first man backed away and thug number two moved in. Dajour kicked him in the stomach, knocking the wind out of him with a loud whoosh. Hit man number three came up from behind and flung a meaty arm around Dajour's neck.

Dajour wiggled free just as the first guy recovered. In a sudden, blurry explosion of speed one of the man's fists connected with Dajour's jaw. Dajour took about five punches and five kicks in roughly four seconds and felt his legs give way. As he fell to his hands and knees one of the men booted him in the stomach.

Grace left her high heeled shoes on the sidewalk outside the club and ran for the parking garage across the street. Drivers flashed their lights and honked, but she darted through four lanes of traffic without looking. She hesitated at the garage entrance, realizing she had no idea where the valet had parked the Bentley. A pair of sawhorses blocked the down ramp and some instinct told her to go in that direction.

She saw the Bentley first, then Dajour on his knees with a man kicking him. Grace flung herself into the air and landed on one the man's back. Clinging to his neck with one arm, she beat his head with her purse.

"Get off me, you stupid bitch!" He brushed her away like a troublesome mosquito and she landed on the hood of the car, then rolled onto the pavement. Stunned, she began crawling toward Dajour.

Dajour saw the next kick coming out of the corner of his eye. He grabbed the man's ankle and twisted, bringing him down. Headlights arced against the wall at the bottom of the ramp.

"Finish him off and let's go!" one of the men shouted."

A knife blade gleamed in the light. Dajour tried to roll under the car, but one of the men grabbed him. The last thing he saw was Grace crawling toward him, crying and calling his name.

The men's footsteps clanged on the metal staircase. Grace pulled herself to her feet and staggered toward Dajour as a car stopped beside them.

"Oh my God!" a woman said as she hopped out of the passenger side.

"Call an ambulance!" someone shouted.

Grace knelt beside Dajour, who was curled in a fetal position with both hands clutching his stomach. She straightened him out and screamed again. Blood gushed from a wound in his throat, spewing from his neck with each heartbeat. A man from the car threw her a hand towel and she stuffed it inside the wound.

Dajour coughed up a mouthful of blood. "Booby, I love you."

"Shhhh, baby. Don't try to talk." People crowded around her, but Grace focused only on Dajour. "Please don't die," she pleaded. "Don't leave me, Dajour. I'm so sorry."

The ambulance arrived quickly and the paramedics took over. A man helped her stand and tried to lead her away, but she wouldn't leave Dajour's side until they loaded him into the ambulance. When she tried to climb in after him the driver moved her aside and slammed the door. "Sorry lady, but we can't take you with us. It's against the rules."

"Grace, stand back so they can leave." Someone tugged at her elbow and she spun around. There stood the woman from the jewelry store. Grace's tangled emotions coalesced into pure hatred. "You bitch! What are you doing here? This whole thing is your fault!" She lunged at Roxanne, but lost her balance and nearly fell.

"I just came down on the elevator to leave something in your car. I had no idea you were here."

"I'm sure you didn't, you slut. I know what you've been doing with Dajour."

"You're so busy looking for trouble you don't even know your own man." Roxanne opened her purse, pulled out a folder, and dropped it at Grace's feet. "Read this and you'll understand." Without another word she walked away.

As the crowd dispersed, mumbling and looking back at her, Grace scooped the items from the floor: A booklet entitled Weddings by Roxanne. A business card clipped to a handful of receipts—including one from a jewelry store. Honeymoon packages, invitation designs, a checklist, and two airplane tickets. Hands trembling, Grace unfolded the tickets. They were made out to Grace and Dajour Wright. The last item on the checklist, in Dajour's handwriting, read "Propose to Grace."

CHAPTER 15

Grace stood beside the car for what seemed like hours, but it must've been only a few minutes before a police officer approached her. It was Sergeant Barney, the woman who'd been there when Smitty was hurt.

"Miss Johnson, would you like a ride to the hospital?"

In the patrol car Grace put her head back and closed her eyes. The back seat smelled of cigarettes, sweat, and fear. With her blood soaked dress and bare feet, Grace figured she just added to the ambience. Sergeant Barney let her ride up front. She leaned her head against the doorframe and watched the streets roll past, picturing how Dajour had tried to smile when she leaned over him. The radio crackled and spit out information that meant nothing to her.

"Do you think he'll be all right? She asked the policewoman.

"You want the truth?"

Grace nodded. "I guess so."

"A bleeder like that—it's usually touch and go. Looked to me like they slit his jugular vein."

Grace pressed on her neck with one hand, as though that would somehow help Dajour cling to life.

At the hospital the desk clerk offered a scrub suit and led her to a bathroom near the ER where she could change clothes and wash her hands. She wadded up the dress and stuffed it into the waste basket, then pulled on the pale green uniform and hurried back to the ER.

She spotted Dajour through the open door of the trauma room, lying on a cot surrounded by nurses and doctors. His mahogany skin glistened under the bright lights and a white sheet covered him from the waist down. Half a dozen machines surrounded him, plus a gigantic red toolbox with the drawers gaping open. She recognized the same ER doctor who'd worked on Smitty.

"Vitals?" the doctor snapped.

"BP eighty over zip, pulse one hundred and forty, respirations twenty-eight," a nurse called out.

"Increase the fluids and blood." The doctor looked up briefly. "Have we got the type and cross-match?"

"We're losing him!" Regular beeps from the heart monitor changed to a steady, high pitched buzz. A nurse called out, "He's gone into V fib!"

The team went into action, placing more equipment on Dajour's body, giving drugs, shoving a tube down his throat. A silver haired nurse spotted Grace watching from the doorway and rushed over to shut the door. "You don't need to see this, honey We'll come and talk to you in a few minutes."

Grace wandered into the waiting area where a group of Dajour's friends and family had gathered. They led her to a chair in the corner and she sat with her head bowed and arms folded across her chest. Conversations went on above her head, but she couldn't speak or even understand what people were saying.

Someone touched her arm—the police detective again. "Grace, we're looking for the men who did this and you're the one who saw them up close. Can you talk to me for a few minutes?"

Sergeant Barney led her into a private room and shut the door behind them. Grace sank into a brocade chair and the policewoman sat opposite her, so close their knees almost touched, and took a notebook from her pocket. She wore a dark brown double breasted suit over a black T-shirt. Her gold shield hung from black nylon cord around her neck.

"I know you're in shock and all that, but we need to catch these guys. Are you with me?"

Grace nodded. "I want to help, but I didn't see much. The men had their backs to me and then I jumped on one of them. After he threw me off I stayed on the floor trying to reach Dajour. I didn't look up."

"You can call me Marcella." The sergeant stripped off a twist of foil from a pack of gum and removed one stick. "Gum?" She extended the package to Grace.

"No thanks." Grace stared at the floor, still picturing Dajour on the table and that shrill sound from the heart monitor.

"Any reason to think someone had a grudge against Dajour?"

Grace realized she was in trouble. She wanted the men arrested, but wouldn't they lead the police directly to Mason, and then to her? She needed to throw the police off until she could decide what to do. "How about Low, the man Dajour fired?"

"No." Marcella tapped her pen against the notebook. "This case is entirely different. In fact, I suspect it's a professional job from the way they set things up. Someone blocked off the lower level of the garage, shut down the elevators, and made sure your car was parked there." She popped a stick of gum into her mouth. "Have you and Dajour been getting along okay?"

When Janet saw a commotion near the front door and heard sirens outside the nightclub, she feared the worst. She looked around for Mason, who'd been across the room partying with a couple of women, but he'd disappeared—probably through the back door. She fought her way through the crowd and reached the front entrance in time to see an ambulance swing into the parking garage across the street.

"What's going on?" she asked the bouncer, a huge Samoan guy with a topknot.

"Somebody got beat up, I think. Happens all the time."

Not to my friends, Janet thought. Along with several other curious people she crossed the street and walked down the ramp where a crowd had already gathered. She gasped.

Dajour lay on the cement floor while EMTs scrambled to start and IV and stem the bleeding from a wound on his neck. A police woman held Grace's arm to keep her back.

"He's gonna die," the man beside her said. "Nobody can lose that much blood and survive."

She wanted to approach Grace and find out what had happened, but didn't dare go any closer with the police hanging around. In fact, officers were moving through the crowd, asking people if they'd seen what happened. She slunk away before Grace noticed her.

Now she stood outside the emergency room entrance at the hospital, having learned from the family that Dajour's life hung by a thread. She immediately called Mason's cell phone.

"Mason, what happened? They're saying Dajour could die! I thought you were just going to rough him up, nothing serious?"

"Well, I revised the plan after we talked. We both wanted him out of the way, so why not have it done right?"

"What if he dies?"

Mason chuckled. "Then we'll take good care of Grace, won't we? I can see myself living in that house and you'll be her best friend."

"Who said anything about you and Grace getting together? That ain't gonna happen."

"You're wrong. Just think about it. If you say one word—one single word—against me to Grace, I'll see you end up in jail for this assault."

Janet nearly threw the phone across the parking lot, but she controlled herself. "Mason, you'll be sorry. I've known Grace a lot longer than you have. She won't fall for your stupid line."

"You did."

"You sneaky bastard!" Janet clicked her phone off before he could respond. Now she had to deal with Mason before he had a chance to work on Grace.

Marcella's questions became more pointed and the woman's dark eyes seemed to look right into Grace's soul. "So, it looks like I'll be questioning your friends and employees over the next few days. Is there anything you want to tell me now?"

"I don't see what our relationship has to do with this," Grace said. "We love each other."

"Hmmm," Marcella answered.

A piercing scream echoed down the hallway. Grace and Marcella charged out of the conference room and back to the ER. In the waiting room Dajour's mother had thrown herself backwards, held by her two young nephews.

"My baby! My baby!" she shouted.

Grace and Marcella caught the doctor outside the trauma room. He shut the door firmly behind him so they couldn't see inside, but Grace caught a glimpse of bloody towels piled on the floor. "What happened?" she asked.

"I'm sorry, but we couldn't save Mr. Wright. He lost several pints of blood from the neck wound before he got here.

Besides that, he had a ruptured spleen and three fractured ribs. One of the ribs punctured his left lung. With so many strikes against him, he just couldn't make it."

Grace watched the doctor's mouth but the words didn't seem to make sense. Suddenly she saw two doctors and the room rotated around her. She felt Marcella's strong arms, then everything went black.

CHAPTER 16

Dajour's murder made the local newspapers for a few days, but the reporters went on to other things when they couldn't gain access to the estate. Grace hid inside the house and stayed in bed for two days, wearing one of Dajour's shirts she'd taken from the laundry hamper, hugging his pillow, and crying until her stomach ached. Janet and Mason stopped by, but she had Maria send them away. She refused to speak with anyone but her parents. Mama was busy taking care of Daddy, but she called every day.

Grace arranged to have Dajour's funeral at the Mount Zion Methodist Church, the red brick church he'd wanted to attend. Miss Carlotta objected at first, but Grace's money won the day. Over a hundred mourners packed the sanctuary for the funeral service. Grace joined Dajour's family on the front row, but they mostly ignored her. Smitty and Doretha hugged her and sat in the back with Dajour's other friends. She noticed Janet, who waved and settled back to fan herself with a program. Folks she didn't know crowded the small church—people Dajour had befriended over the years, including a clerk from the convenience store near their old apartment, his ex-boss, and a dozen residents from the old neighborhood.

Almost everyone had something to say about Dajour's life and the service dragged on for two hours. Grace felt sick to her stomach and dizzy because she hadn't eaten. Seemed like she was stuck in a bad movie that would never end. It just couldn't be her life; not without Dajour in it.

The last person to speak was Roxanne. Grace sucked in her breath as the young woman looked directly at her and said, "I didn't wear red today, but some people seemed to think I should."

Grace had rented a limousine for the day so she could go to the cemetery in a car by herself. The driver, who introduced himself as Frank, wore a tailored uniform, kept his eyes on the road, and had enough sense not to attempt conversation. She wanted to lie down in the seat and sleep, but first she had to survive one more ordeal—the burial.

Miss Charletta fell apart and had to be carried off when they lowered Dajour's casket into the ground. Grace dropped a single red rose into the grave, then turned and walked toward her car.

She left the main path and wandered through the old part of the cemetery, giving the crowd time to leave. She barely glanced at the tombstones as she passed them, but something special caught her eye. Standing atop a flat marble stone was a beautifully carved statue of a little girl. The girl wore an old fashioned pinafore with her hair twisted into braids. Her expression was solemn. A bush bearing yellow roses grew in front of the tombstone and someone had left flowers in a cut glass vase.

The inscription on the headstone read "In loving memory of Francine Nixon, our little angel."

Francine. That name sounded familiar. Grace circled the stone. On the back she noticed a photograph embedded in the marble. She glanced at it, then looked closer. Finally, she knelt on the grass beside the stone and peered into the little girl's face. It was the same girl she'd talked to in the park—the one who gave her Raggedy Ann.

Janet had waited all through the funeral and the graveside

service for a few minutes alone with Grace. To her annoyance, Grace wandered into the graveyard and she was stuck exchanging pleasantries with Smitty and his wife. She kept one eye on Grace while discussing what a wonderful person Dajour had been and how much he'd be missed.

Yeah, he would be missed, but mostly Janet worried about her own neck.

Grace spotted Janet coming in her direction as she climbed into the limousine, with Frank holding the door for her. Janet was the last person on earth she wanted to see, but it didn't seem right to just drive off and leave her standing there. So she waved Frank aside and waited.

Janet trotted across the grass, gasping for breath. "Whew, I'm so out of shape." She fanned herself with one hand. "Grace, I've been trying to reach you all week. We need to talk."

"About what?" Grace turned and shaded her eyes against the afternoon sun.

"About Mason and what happened to Dajour," Janet hissed. She glanced at the thinning crowd, but no one paid them any attention. "I want you to know I had no idea what Mason was planning. None of this is my fault—and I hope you realize that."

Grace stopped walking. "Are you saying Mason *meant* to have Dajour killed?"

"I thought you'd have figured that out by now. Did you think using the knife was a last minute decision?"

"Why would Mason do that?"

"He wants your money. Everyone wants your money. Mason's thinks he's either going to marry you or blackmail you—whichever is easiest."

Grace waved the chauffeur aside and leaned against the car. She couldn't bear to look at Janet's face, nor could she look at the mound of dirt surrounding Dajour's grave. Instead she stared at a row of treetops in the distance. "Janet, I think you're in this up to your neck. Dajour tried to warn me, but I wouldn't listen."

Janet's face turned ugly. "If one of us goes down, we all three go. Just remember that, you snobbish bitch. And you won't be able to redecorate in jail."

Stunned, Grace climbed into the car and told the chauffeur to take the long way back to town. If Mason had planned to kill Dajour, then she'd been party to a murder. A murder that would never have happened without her jealousy and suspicion.

The tears she hadn't shed at the funeral suddenly began flowing. She lay in the seat and soaked the upholstery with her tears. What was the use of going back to the empty mansion by herself? She couldn't buy love. In fact, she'd already sold out the best love she'd ever found.

Grace tapped on the divider to get the driver's attention and moments later the glass slid apart a few inches.

"Yes, Ma'am?"

"Frank, take me to the nearest police station."

He turned down the music. "Did you say police station?"

"Yes. The nearest one."

He turned onto a side street and entered a neighborhood that featured empty storefronts, seedy looking taverns, and drug dealers slinking around on the sidewalks. Frank stopped in front of a brick building with several police cars parked out front. "You're sure this is where you want to go? I can take you to a better police station."

"This is perfect," Grace got out of the car and handed him a roll of bills. "You keep that money, because I won't need it."

She climbed the steps without looking back and

approached an young officer behind the front desk. He glanced up and laid a crossword puzzle aside.

"May I help you?" He raised an eyebrow, looking at Grace's expensive dress.

She set her purse on the desk and took a deep breath. "I killed my boyfriend and I had help setting it up."

CHAPTER 17

Mason searched his bedroom for the car keys. He distinctly remembered leaving them on the kitchen counter, but they'd disappeared—along with half his brain cells. Lately his mind was so rattled he couldn't keep track of anything.

That nasty woman detective had arrested him shortly after Grace turned herself in. The police were none too gentle and Sergeant Barney looked like she wanted to cut his balls off. They kept him in a hot, smelly holding cell for 8 hours before his attorney arrived.

Mason smiled, picturing the look on Barney's face when he presented his "Get Out of Jail Free" card—the Ukrainian connection. The FBI desperately wanted anything they could get on the Russian Mafia, and Mason knew enough to get himself out on bail and arrange a plea bargain. Thanks to the high priced lawyer it wasn't likely he'd spend any time in jail.

He smoothed his hair in front of the mirror on the dresser. Damn, but he did look fine. Having his picture on the front page of the Washington Post turned out to be excellent publicity money for the business. So many clients lined up for his services that he'd taken on a second assistant. Another bonus: the minute he showed his face in the nightclubs, women swarmed all over him.

He straightened his tie and continue searching. After checking the bathroom, he finally found his keys in the jacket he'd worn the day before. By now he was late for his first appointment, but the client would wait. Balancing a cup of coffee in one hand and his attaché case in the other, he armed the security system, locked the apartment, and took the elevator to the parking garage.

"Morning, Harold. Anything new?"

"Morning, Mr. Mason. Same old, same old." The elderly security guard grinned at him over the morning paper.

The Mustang waited in one corner of the garage like a beautiful woman, sleek and sexy. Life was good. Mason set his coffee in the holder, careful not to spill anything on the leather upholstery. He turned the key in the ignition. And then, he heard the *click*. His eyes opened wide in bewilderment. The parking garage had security guards 24 hours a day. They'd never had a break in. How could, how could...

Stay calm, Mason told himself. You can handle this. Simply slip out of the car, hit the ground, and roll.

The electrical current from the car's starter box reached the electrical ignition switch of the bomb and Mason's car exploded into a thousand flaming pieces.

Three blocks away, Grace sat in the cafeteria of the county detention center along with fifty or sixty other women. Breakfast consisted of runny scrambled eggs, white bread, and two limp slices of bacon.

The slight tremor was unmistakable. "Did you feel that?" one of the guards asked.

The inmates looked at each other and a frowsy blonde woman nudged Grace in the ribs. "Somebody's done blowed up something."

A few minutes later, the harsh sound of screaming sirens cut the air.

"Must've been something big," Grace added.

The next morning Grace met with her attorney in a tiny room at the Central Detention Facility. She wore an orange jumpsuit and her hair hadn't been washed or combed since she entered jail. She shuffled into the room, slumped in the metal chair, and heaved a deep sigh. All she wanted to do was sleep.

Adrienne Rich, her attorney, slid the Washington Post across the table. "Grace, I wanted to be the one to tell you—Mason's dead."

"You're kidding?" Grace sat up straight. "What happened?"

"Somebody planted a bomb in his car and it blew up yesterday morning. I doubt they'll find enough pieces to give him a decent burial."

Grace was silent for a moment. "The Ukrainians?"

Adrienne nodded, then glanced at the microphone above their heads. "Street talk says the three guys are on their way to Odessa, but there's no way they'd let Mason get away with ratting on them."

"I thought Mason was smarter than that." Grace said, examining her nails to hide her smile.

"I guess Mason's death isn't a big loss to you."

"He got what he deserved. But what about Janet? Did you find out what happened to her?"

"Without your support she lost the business—especially after those phone calls you had me make. She's working as a bank teller and already having an affair with her manager, who's married."

"You'll take care of that, right?"

"Sure, that's what you pay me for. Janet won't last long in that job." Adrienne opened a folder and removed a sheaf of papers. "We really need to discuss your own case, Grace. You're in the headlines every day—especially after this thing with Mason. Your case even made the national news."

"Why does anyone care about me?"

"Because your rich, beautiful, and you allegedly had your boyfriend killed. Also, you're pleading guilty and you won't let me fight for you. You wouldn't even ask for bail. This is big news. You've become a celebrity."

Grace glanced at the paper. Somewhere they'd found a photo of her with Dajour, the two of them smiling at the camera. Below that was a shot of Mason. "Exactly what is it you think I should do?"

"Look at me, Grace." Adrienne tapped her fingers on the table. "Listen up. We see the judge tomorrow and it's your last chance. I can get you off with a fairly light sentence, especially if we plea bargain and you testify against Mason and Janet. Please let me do my job! You'll be out on good behavior within a few years."

Grace smiled and shook her head. "Can't you see I'm exactly where I belong?"

The next morning a superior court judge sentenced Grace to life without parole. Reporters and photographers swarmed the courthouse steps and gathered around Attorney Rich as she left the building. Grace simply went back to the Central Detention Center and awaited transport to her new home—a prison where she'd spend the rest of her life.

That's when the dreams started. Every night Grace walked down a long aisle wearing a beautiful white satin wedding dress and a lace veil. She carried a bouquet of pink roses. Roses, lilacs, and wild flowers framed the alter where Pastor Milloy awaited her. She passed Roxanne, her mother and father, Smitty and Doretha, and all their friends and acquaintances. Tears of joy ran down her mother's face and even Miss Charletta dabbed at her eyes with a lace handkerchief. When Grace's father stood to give her away he looked healthy and strong.

Dajour took her hands and they mouthed the words "I do."

That's when she would awaken to the sounds of the prison at night. Women crying, metal doors slamming shut, a toilet flushing. She'd rise and pace the floor until morning; ten steps forward, ten steps back.

Lisa Chang snapped off the tape recorder. Although Grace had talked nonstop for almost two hours, one question still remained. "Grace, why did you do it? You had everything!"

Grace gave her the saddest smile she'd ever seen. "I honestly don't know. Maybe when I figure that out I'll stop having the dreams."

Lisa gathered her paperwork into a pile. "Well, I can't think of anything else to ask you at the moment. I'll send the first draft of the manuscript in a few weeks. Will you write to me?" She asked the question absently, still focused on her notes.

Grace didn't respond. She was staring across the room, her mouth hanging open.

A glimmering ball of light hovered above the floor for a few seconds and then expanded, growing even more radiant. For an instant Lisa saw—or thought she saw—a girl in a frilly pink dress. When Lisa closed her eyes and looked again, the hallucination was gone. But she distinctly heard a girl's voice say, "Grace, God will help you."

Grace's eyes rolled back in her head and she slumped forward, bashing her head on the metal table. Lisa rushed around the table to catch her before she slid to the floor. An alarm sounded overhead and three guards charged into the room.

"Get back!"

"I think she just fainted," Lisa said as the guards carried

Grace from the room. She looked around, expecting people to be agitated and excited about the apparition, but everyone calmly resumed their conversations. Only a little boy carrying a dirty flannel blanket seemed interested. Dragging his blanket, he waddled to the corner where the light had appeared. He giggled, spun around, and held out his hands as though playing with an invisible friend.

Lisa decided mentioning her experience to the guards didn't seem like a good idea; they were already giving her strange looks. She wasn't sure what just happened, but she wanted out—and fast.

As she tossed the legal pad into her attaché case she spotted a Raggedy Ann doll under the table. A stuffed toy wasn't something they allowed inside the prison, so she had no idea how the doll made it past the checkpoints. Without looking back Lisa grabbed her case, stuffed the doll inside, and hurried out the door.

The little boy's high pitched laughter followed her down the hallway.